Linguistic Foundations
for
Reading

Other Books of Interest:

Linguistic Foundations for Reading

MaryAnne Hall
Georgia State University

Christopher J. Ramig
Georgia State University

Charles E. Merrill Publishing Company
A Bell & Howell Company
Columbus   Toronto   London   Sydney

Published by
Charles E. Merrill Publishing Company
A Bell & Howell Company
Columbus, Ohio 43216

LB1050
H27

This book was set in Times Roman.
The Production Editor was Sharon Keck Thomason.
The cover was prepared by Will Chenoweth.

Library of Congress Catalog Card Number: 77-80093
International Standard Book Number: 0-675-08448-2

Printed in the United States of America
1 2 3 4 5 6 7 8 9 / 82 81 80 79 78

Contents

Preface

The impetus for *Linguistic Foundations for Reading* grew from an awareness of the increasing amount of and emphasis on linguistic information about reading in recent years. The book also grew from a concern that linguistic information that would be valuable to the teacher of reading was often ignored because the application seemed elusive, nebulous, nonexistent, and/or overwhelming since teachers felt inadequate in linguistic background to comprehend or apply that information. In this book we seek to examine linguistic foundations for reading and to clarify how those foundations can be applied to improve the teaching of reading. This book grew too from concern that linguistic suggestions for reading may have ignored the child. The concern expressed in this book is that the child, the linguistic nature of the reading process, and instructional procedures must be meshed to produce effective learning of the skills of literacy. Along with the sound linguistic base for reading instruction, we seek to offer a humanistic view of language and of language learning.

A linguistic perspective for reading instruction is presented in chapter 1, the nature of language is described in chapter 2, the language learner is the topic of chapter 3, and the relationship between spoken and written language is the focus of chapter 4. Chapter 5 discusses phonology and orthography, and chapter 6 examines comprehension from its syntactical and semantic bases. In both chapters 5 and 6, guidelines for instruction are featured. The purpose of chapter 7 is to highlight applications from linguistics to classroom practices.

As we became more aware of linguistic knowledge, we also became aware that much of what was done in teaching reading was inaccurate and unjustifiable from a linguistic base. We also realized that much of what was being done in the teaching of reading was justifiable from a linguistic base but that teachers were unaware of the linguistic rationale of many procedures that they found effective.

At this writing, the linguistic foundation for reading is not yet complete, and the coming years should add much to the material presented here. It is our hope that in the future educators will be receptive to linguistic information so that the communication gap between education and linguistics that was characteristic in prior years will no longer be an obstacle to developing better instruction for children.

The content reflected here is that which has resulted from our continuing search for understanding of the reading process stemming from our experiences as classroom teachers and from our work with prospective and inservice teachers in courses in the teaching of reading. Our linguistic perspective is an educator's perspective on reading and language learning.

A Linguistic
Perspective
for Reading

One premise upon which this book is based is that effective reading instruction must embody not only sound pedagogical principles but must also be founded upon the most accurate and appropriate linguistic information that is currently available. We believe that reading is a means of communication through language and that as such language and reading are inextricably intertwined. Thus, a teacher's knowledge about various aspects of language will influence the strategies employed to help children master the process of reading and will affect instruction in the related communication skills of listening, speaking, and writing. What teachers integrate from linguistics with sound pedagogy is, in our opinion, critical to the success of their teaching of reading and to the learning of their students.

In this chapter, linguistics and reading are defined, and the influence of linguistic study on reading is discussed. Attention is paid to both the contributions and limitations of linguistics for the teaching of reading. The intent of this chapter is to provide a linguistic perspective for reading. Subsequent chapters provide more detailed information and present discussion of specific implications of the linguistic perspective for instruction.

How Is Linguistics Defined?

Linguistics is the scientific inquiry of language, its form, structure, and function. Linguists study language for the purposes of examining the ways in which features of a particular language serve to promote communication and understanding the "nature of human language and the processes of its functioning."[1] According to Whitney,

[1]Charles C. Fries, *Linguistics and Reading* (New York: Holt, Rinehart and Winston, 1963), p. 36.

"To assemble, arrange, and explain the whole body of linguistic phenomona, so as throughly to comprehend them, in each separate part and under all aspects, is [the linguist's] endeavor."[2] Linguistics is a science in which all aspects of language provide the raw material that linguists study.

Although humankind has always been interested in language, the scientific study of language dates from the first quarter of the 19th century. Between 1825 and the present, advances in linguistics have proceeded somewhat in stages or periods related to the theoretical assumptions under examination as well as to advances in procedure and methodology.

Historically, linguistics has been broadly conceived, and throughout its history various issues have come to be refined, redefined, and resolved or, in some cases, considered either unanswerable or irrelevant. That which is of contemporary relevancy is determined by the theoretical framework and set of hypotheses which have been derived through examination of previously accumulated knowledge and are currently assumed to be appropriate. For example, during the seventeenth, eighteenth, and nineteenth centuries, interest in describing vernacular European languages and writing descriptive grammars for these languages increased among linguists replacing, at least somewhat, prescriptions of correct usage based on a Latin model. Today linguists, while still concerned with such traditional philosophical issues as the relationship between thought and language, are interested in developmental aspects of language acquisition and the educational implications of social class and dialect differences in language.

Linguistics has never been narrowly defined, nor has the range of scientific activity of the linguist been narrowly conceived. There is virtually no aspect of language and, consequently no aspect of human life, that linguistics fails to consider in some manner.

Fries defined linguistics as

> . . . a body of knowledge and understanding concerning the nature and functioning of human language, built up out of information about the structure, the operation, and the history of a wide range of very diverse human languages[3]

Linguistics as a science today is concerned with the history and development of language in a branch of linguistics called *historical linguistics*. It is also concerned with similarities and differences among languages (comparative linguistics), the structure of language (structural linguistics), and with the ways in which language is related to thinking (psycholinguistics). Within these various branches, moreover, lie semantics, phonetics, rhetoric, dialectology, syntax, the study of usage, the study of written language, lexicology, and etymology.

Reading and reading instruction have not escaped nor should they escape the linguist's examination. The linguist employs a set of tools and a scientific procedure for the examination of language through which a perspective for reading and reading instruction has developed and from which insights into the nature of reading and reading instruction have emanated.

---

[2]William Dwight Whitney, *Language and the Study of Language: Twelve Lectures on the Principles of Linguistic Science,* Charles Scribner and Co., 1867, preface, pp. vii-viii. Cited in Charles C. Fries, *Linguistics and Reading* (New York: Holt, Rinehart and Winston, Inc., 1963), p. 42.
[3]Charles C. Fries, *Linguistics and Reading* (New York: Holt Rinehart and Winston), 1963, p. 91.

How Is Reading Defined?

Of fundamental importance in describing and discussing the linguistic foundations upon which reading instruction should be based is an understanding of the nature of the reading process. According to Gray, sound reading instruction and the development of reading programs "presupposes a clear understanding of the nature of reading and the fundamental processes involved."[4] We should like to point out, however, that there is not universal agreement on the nature of reading. Otto commented:

> Conceptions of 'reading', then, range from extremely narrow to extremely broad; they are confined to the decoding of printed symbols and basic oral responses at one extreme and they move through the grasping of literal meaning and the interpretation of ideas to the inclusion of changes in behavior that result from decoding at the other extreme.[5]

To illustrate this lack of agreement, let us consider several definitions of reading and discuss the implications of these definitions for reading instruction. One of the narrower definitions states that

> Reading is first of all, and essentially, the mechanical skill of decoding, of turning the printed symbols into the sounds which are language. Of course the reason we turn the print into sound, (that is, read) is to get at the meaning. We decode the printed symbols in order to hear what they "say."[6]

Reading defined in this manner implies instructional practices which place emphasis upon accuracy in decoding written words into their oral counterparts. Letter-sound relationships are presented by the teacher, rehearsed by the children, then practiced through the oral reading of materials that contain these letter-sound patterns. Unfortunately, this oral reading is often done without prior silent reading and carried out in small groups in which each child takes a turn reading a portion of the material orally, a procedure commonly called "round robin" reading. In reading instruction following this sort of procedure, attention to meaning is minimal in contrast to that of attention to accuracy in sound-pattern–letter-pattern correspondences.

Reading programs developed from this conceptualization of reading include a sequenced presentation of letter-sound correspondence or spelling-pattern–sound-pattern relationships. Children are taught these relationships in the order in which they appear in this predetermined sequence. Mastery of the ability to decode these spelling patterns to oral language is thought to be rewarding in itself for the beginning reader.

A second definition of reading is built upon the study of the interrelationships between language and thought–psycholinguistics. Goodman viewed reading as a psycholinguistic process.

---

[4]William S. Gray, *The Teaching of Reading: A Second Report,* Part I of *The Thirty-sixth Yearbook of the National Society for the Study of Education* (Bloomington, Illinois: Public School Publishing Company, 1937), pp. 25–28.

[5]Wayne Otto, "Reading Behavior: Fact or Artifact—," *Journal of Reading Behavior* 2 (Summer, 1970): 224.

[6]Glenn McCracken and Charles C. Walcutt, *Basic Reading.* Reader 1-1 and Reader 1-2, Teacher's Edition (Philadelphia: J.B. Lippincott, 1963), p. iv.

It involves partial use of available minimal language cues selected from perceptual in-put on the basis of the reader's expectation. As this partial information is processed, tentative decisions are made to be confirmed, rejected, or refined as reading pro-gresses.[7]

Goodman offered a succinct definition when he described reading as the reconstruc-tion of a message from print.[8]

In a psycholinguistic conceptualization of reading, such as Goodman's, efficient reading occurs when the reader gains skill in selecting the least but most productive information from written language necessary to make good guesses about the meaning of the message. This view of reading implies classroom practices in which si-lent, rather than oral, reading would be emphasized and in which meaning, rather than precision in producing oral counterparts to spelling patterns, would be of highest priority. In such a classroom, teachers would use reading materials including content reflective of the experiences of the reader and written in language (syntactic) patterns similar to those of the reader's. Use of context clues, both semantic (meaning) and syntactic (grammatical), would be the primary word identification strategy emphasized. Also in instruction based on this view, a significant portion of time spent in the reading of meaningful literature would be emphasized.

A third way of defining reading includes a principal role for cognitive processes. Stauffer described reading as a thinking process as follows:

> Reading is a mental process—a dynamic, active way of performing—and it can be taught that way. It is a mental process in the sense that it is of the mind, that it is cognitive.[9]

Conceptualizing reading in this way makes paramount the cognitive, or thinking, as-pects not only of reading itself but also of reading instruction. Classroom instruction practices which are implied by such a conceptualization would include helping children establish purposes for reading, facilitating reasoning as children are reading, promot-ing evaluation or judgment, and encouraging children to relect upon, refine, and extend the ideas they have encountered in their reading.

Children, directed toward meaning by the milieu of the classroom and by the teacher, would use the search for meaning to direct the entire reading process. Reading is conducted for the purpose of answering self-generated questions, although at first children must learn to generate the questions, and is focused on understanding and re-flection. Word identification strategies become the result of a need to know rather than the step at which all children must be at a given point in a sequence of reading "skills."

Something of a synthesis of the psycholinguistic definition of Goodman and the cognitive view of Stauffer is reflected in our definition of reading: *Reading is the pro-cessing of written language symbols so as to arrive at a meaningful interpretation of an author's intentions, attitudes, beliefs, and/or feelings.*

Classroom practices that are implied by this definition include a thorough and on-going emphasis on experiences with written language in which the primary objective

[7]Kenneth S. Goodman, "Reading: A Psycholinguistic Guessing Game," *Journal of the Reading Specialist* 4 (May, 1967):126-27.

[8]Kenneth S. Goodman, *The Psycholinguistic Nature of the Reading Process* (Detroit: Wayne State University Press, 1968), p. 15.

[9]Russell G. Stauffer, *Directing the Reading-Thinking Process* (New York: Harper and Row, Inc., 1975), p. 6.

and overriding concern is the acquisition of meaning. All written language used in reading instruction must involve experience, intentions, attitudes, beliefs, and/or feelings that are potentially meaningful to the reader, thus emphasizing the communicative function of language and language processing.

Unfortunately, many reading instructional materials and an overwhelmingly large number of classroom practices in the teaching of reading are employed by classroom teachers with little or no regard for the theoretical or definitional view of reading which underlies the instruction. While this may be the result of lack of participation in the process of selecting material, it may also be simply a lack of knowledge of differences in the rationale that underlies one set of materials and the rationale that underlies another set. The problem such a lack of analysis of material or lack of understanding of rationale leads to is often manifested in inappropriate or erroneous classroom instruction. Teachers should have better reason for teaching something than "That's what the manual said to do" since what the manual says may be linguistically inaccurate or pedagogically inappropriate.

In subsequent chapters, we will elaborate on the classroom implications we see for our definition of reading. These practices are rigorously based in the communicative and cognitive aspects of language and are founded in our assumption of a linguistic base for reading instruction.

Although we believe that the cognitive foundations for reading are as important as the linguistic foundations, our intent in this book is to examine the linguistic base for reading. However, because the linguistic and the cognitive underpinnings for reading are interrelated, the cognitive base will be considered where it is appropriate.

The Development of Linguistic Influence on Reading

Attention to linguistic study and its relevance to the teaching of reading was not generally evident until after the midcentury mark of the 1900s. The number of articles and books dealing with the applications of linguistics to classroom settings has increased significantly since 1950. Hodges and Rudorf noted that it was not until the mid 1950s that linguists considered the implications of their work for schools—or vice versa. [10] The decade of the sixties brought considerable attention to the discussion of linguistic findings to the teaching of reading. Rystrom observed that although the study of American linguistics can be traced back to the work of Bloomfield and Fries in the early thirties, it was not until the sixties that teachers became seriously interested in the potential applications of linguistics to the teaching of reading. [11] However, much of this interest has led to the labeling of materials or programs as "linguistic" without sufficient concern for informing teachers of reading of the assumptions about language and reading on which these instructional programs were based.

Leonard Bloomfield, who is credited with creating the first linguistic stir in the reading field, maintained that, "To understand reading one must understand the relation

---

[10]Richard E. Hodges and E. Hugh Rudorf, *Language and Learning to Read* (Boston: Houghton Mifflin Company, 1972), p.5.

[11]Richard Rystrom, "Linguistics and the Teaching of Reading," *Journal of Reading Behavior 4* (Winter 1972) :34.

of written (or printed) words to speech." [12] He believed that, especially for beginning readers, major emphasis should be on how speech is recorded by written symbols. Bloomfield's interest developed through his efforts in teaching his son to read and from the materials he created for that teaching. These materials were the base for the materials first used in what is commonly called "the linguistic approach." Fries defined reading similarly by stating that "one can 'read' insofar as he can respond to the language signals represented by patterns of graphic shapes as fully as he learned to respond to the same language signals of his code represented by patterns of auditory shapes." [13] For beginning readers, the phoneme–grapheme relationship was stressed while attention to meaning was minimal. Thus, the first linguistic applications to reading instruction were rather narrow and focused primarily on small units of language emphasizing the spelling patterns and the phoneme-grapheme relationships of the language.

A differing emphasis was expressed by another linguist, Lefevre, who stated that reading requires "recognition of graphic counterparts of entire spoken utterances, comprehended as unitary meaning—bearing patterns." [14] Two other statements of Lefevre that refer to comprehension are: "Reading is not reading unless it gives access to meaning." [15] "Entire meaning-bearing patterns must be not simply decoded but interpreted and evaluated." [16]

With this change in emphasis from a narrow view of linguistic application to reading to a broad scope with considerable significance has come increased attention to linguistic study. Currently, linguists and educators are concerned with exploring the nature of the language base for reading. There has been a change in emphasis from the narrow view of phoneme–grapheme relationships to analytical descriptions of language and language processing to language use by different groups and the complexities of the interrelation of language and thought.

What Does Linguistics Have to Offer Reading?

We are not advocating a "linguistic method" for reading instruction. Rather we propose that since reading is a language process, all aspects of reading instruction and reading methodology must include appropriate linguistic information. However, a reading-teaching methodology based solely upon linguistic principles would be as equally indefensible as a reading-teaching strategy based solely upon psychological principles. Reading methodology must be based upon accurate linguistic information, but effective instruction must also involve sound psychological principles for meaningful learning to occur. It is neither our intent to deal at length with the psychology of learning, nor to ignore the topic completely. However, the focus is on presenting linguistic information upon which reading instruction can be based for effective reading acquisition to occur.

---

[12]*Leonard Bloomfield and Clarence Barnhart, Let's Read* (Detroit: Wayne State University Press, 1961), p. 19.

[13]Charles C. Fries, *Linguistics and Reading* (New York: Holt, Rinehart and Winston, Inc., 1963) p. 131.

[14]Carl A. Lefevre, *Linguistics and the Teaching of Reading* (New York: McGraw-Hill, 1964), p. 39.

[15]Carl A. Lefevre, "A Multidisciplinary Approach to Language and Reading," in Kenneth S. Goodman, ed. *The Psycholinguistic Nature of the Reading Process* (Detroit: Wayne State University Press, 1968), p. 291.

[16]*Ibid.*, p. 293.

Gathering appropriate linguistic information for reading instruction includes an examination of the nature of language, a probing of how features of language influence a reader's behavior by exploring the reader's language processing strategies, a knowledge of the readers' oral language performance and competence, a consideration of the language patterns included in reading materials, and an identification of teaching behavior that is appropriate within a reading acquisition environment. A linguistic perspective for reading requires that reading be defined as language processing, that the reader be viewed as a user of language, that reading be taught as communication through language, and that teachers understand how language operates in the interaction between the reader and the printed language. Linguistics serves as a source of information that educators can draw upon in developing materials, in selecting appropriate information about language, in devising instructional strategies, and in analyzing the child's performance in the language tasks of reading, writing, speaking, and listening.

Although there are a number of branches of linguistic study, we are most concerned here with the branch often referred to as *applied linguistics*, the application of linguistic principles to educational situations. Two major areas of linguistic study, psycholinguistics and sociolinguistics, are presently having a great deal of impact on the teaching of reading. One concern of psycholinguists is investigation of the learning process in relation to how children learn and use language. Psycholinguists have contributed to the knowledge of how children learn to speak and understand the oral form of language and how they learn to read and write language. Through study of the relationships of thought and language, psycholinguists are adding considerably to the information about reading comprehension. The potential for psycholinguistic impact on reading instruction is noted by Spache.

> The experiments may well have direct implications for vocabulary teaching, for analyzing the cognitive processes underlying comprehension, for the extent and kind of training upon words of structural or lexical function, for adapting our instruction to our knowledge of the fundamental differences between the encoding processes, for new methods of evaluating the reading difficulty of many types of instructional and other materials, for further study of the process of deriving meaning from context, for new approaches to measurement of comprehension and for many other facets of reading.[17]

Ruddell pointed out another manner in which psycholinguistics may serve as a source of information about reading:

> . . . the relationship between psycholinguistics and reading instruction is apparent if one views the former discipline as developing an understanding and explanation of language processing and the latter as having its central focus on the enhancement of the ability to decode and comprehend language.[18]

Applied sociolinguistics also has a body of knowledge and a perspective for inquiry which can provide useful language information to reading teachers. Much of sociolin-

---

[17]George D. Spache, "Contributions of Allied Fields to the Teaching of Reading," *Innovation and Change in Reading Instruction, Part II,* in Helen M. Robinson, ed., *The Sixty-seventh Yearbook of the National Society for the Study of Education* (Chicago: University of Chicago Press, 1968), pp. 271–72.

[18]Robert B. Ruddell, "Psycholinguistic Implications for a System of Communication Model," Harry Singer and Robert B. Ruddell, eds., *Theoretical Models and Processes of Reading* (Newark, Delaware: International Reading Association, 1976), p. 452.

guistics has to do with social class differences in language features and language usage. In reading instruction there is much to be learned from the sociolinguists. For example, the language patterns of the beginning reader may be different from those of the mainstream culture. How does this difference relate to learning to read? What teacher behaviors are appropriate in these circumstances?

In the past, however, a lack of communication between linguists and educators has detracted from the use of much available linguistic information. Wardhaugh claimed that

> it would be true to say that most reading experts have given only token recognition to linguistics in their work, with the consequence that the vast part of what is discussed under the name of linguistics in texts, methods, and courses on reading is in reality very far from the best linguistic knowledge that is available today.[19]

The communication barrier between educators and linguists has been related to educators' rightful resistance to linguists' development of recommendations for teaching without seeking the cooperation of educators and without the consideration of other factors that influence learning and teaching. Educators are concerned that application of linguistic study to the development of effective instructional programs that include a linguistic base and are pedagogically sound is not possible without the educator's perspective. Shane added a perspective:

> The fact that linguists and teachers of reading do not think of reading in the same context does not necessarily imply a conflict; reading theory and methods should be concerned with the strategy and the tactics for employing this information. [20]

Marckwardt emphasized that there needs to be a distinction between the tools and special knowledge that the linguist employs in his discipline and the concepts and conclusions which may usefully be passed on to teachers.[21] Although his comments refer to linguists' contributions to spelling, Venezky's comments seem appropriate for reading as well.

> The linguist can provide for educators data on the pronunciation of English, the nature of the writing system, and the relationship between speech and writing. It is the educator's task, however, to determine which of the linguist's offerings can aid in the teaching of spelling and reading, and how they can be used to achieve this end.[22]

In the study of reading we need to tie linguistic knowledge and teaching strategies together. Moreover, this must be accomplished without the conflict often found in dis-

---

[19]Ronald Wardhaugh, *Reading: A Linguistic Perspective* (New York: Harcourt, Brace and World, 1969), p. 30.

[20]Harold Shane, *Linguistics and the Classroom Teacher* (Washington, D.C. : Association for Supervision and Curriculum Development, 1967), p. 41.

[21]Albert H. Marckwardt, "Introduction," in *Linguistics in School Programs,* Albert H. Marckwardt, ed., *69th Yearbook, National Society for the Study of Education* (Chicago: University of Chicago Press, 1970), p. 1.

[22]Richard L. Venezky, "Linguistics and Spelling," in *Linguistics in School Programs,* Albert H. Marckwardt, ed., *69th Yearbook, National Society for the Study of Education* (Chicago: University of Chicago Press, 1970), pp. 272–73.

cussions of linguistics and reading instruction. Linguists are concerned with exploring knowledge about language and developing language theory while educators are concerned with the application of such knowledge in the development of materials and instructional strategies. Linguistics is a source of information about language, but linguistics is not a source of information about teaching. Although some linguistic study is concerned with language learning (primarily the learning evidenced in the language acquisition process as a child learns to speak his or her native language) linguistics per se does not provide the pedagogical base for teaching and learning.

Research in reading and research in linguistics have generally concentrated on different concerns. As Ives and Ives elaborated

> linguistics deals with knowledge; research in linguistics accumulates information, develops theory based on this information and explains this theory. Reading instruction deals with performance; research in reading studies a kind of behavior and looks for ways to guide this behavior more effectively; courses in reading instruction are largely expositions of methods. The student of language is primarily concerned with factual details and the teacher of reading is primarily concerned with pedagogical strategies. [23]

We contend that the teacher of reading also must concentrate on available linguistic knowledge, without, however, ignoring pedagogical concerns. Linguistics is only one source of information to be incorporated into reading instructional programs, and this information must be integrated with other knowledge to shape curriculum experiences which promote children's facility in communication. While the point of view in this book is that the linguistic foundations of reading are significant, we do not mean to ignore other essentials for effective learning and teaching. A renowned linguist of this century, Noam Chomsky, commented:

> There is a natural enough tendency for teachers to turn to the fundamental disciplines (psychology, linguistics) for guidance, but they should do so with skepticism and a critical attitude. The insights that have been achieved into behavior and mental function are limited. Furthermore, there is little reason to doubt that the dominant factor in successful teaching is and will always remain the teacher's skill in nourishing, and in providing a rich and challenging intellectual environment in which the child can find his own unique way toward understanding, knowledge, and skill. [24]

We feel that Lefevre stated the case well. He wrote that successful teaching of reading and the English language arts require two great ingredients:

> 1. Accurate and up-to-date knowledge of the nature, structure, and functions of the English language.
> 2. Humane teaching, based on the understanding of human growth and development, and the role of language therein. [25]

---

[23]Sumner Ives and Josephine P. Ives, "Linguistics and Reading," in *Linguistics in School Programs,* Albert H. Marckwardt, ed., *69th yearbook, National Society for the Study of Education* (Chicago: University of Chicago Press, 1970), pp. 243–44.

[24]Noam Chomsky, "Phonology and Reading," in *Basic Studies on Reading,* Harry Levin and Joanna P. Williams, eds., (New York: Basic Books, Inc., 1970), p. 3.

[25]Carl A. Lefevre, "Language and Self: Fulfillment or Trauma?" Part II. *Elementary English* 43 (March, 1966):232.

Successful teaching of reading requires an effective teacher—one who is skillful in creating pupil interest, one who provides a learning environment rich in stimulation and warm and accepting in human relationships, and one who bases instructional strategies on appropriate information. There are those who would contend that a linguistic base does little to help the teacher to stimulate children to read. We think that linguistic-based insights about the reading process will add to the overall background a teacher has to offer to students and to the understanding of which procedures and activities are worthwhile in teaching children to perform the language processing tasks essential in reading. A linguistically founded reading program need not overlook pupil interest, motivation, or other components of effective learning. Rather, a linguistically founded reading program will blend justifiable linguistic conclusions with effective instruction.

Concluding Statement

It is incumbent that in seeking to develop accurate foundations for reading and to have reading instruction built on an understanding of how language functions in the reading process, we examine the major implications of linguistic scholarship for reading instruction and narrow the gulf between linguistic research and its potential contributions to the teaching of reading and other communication skills. The need in reading instruction is to use linguistic information in the development of theories of learning to read and in developing strategies for teaching children to function at their maximum levels in developing their communication potential. Subsequent chapters will provide information derived from linguistics and suggest specific methodological use of this information.

Suggested Readings

Deese, James. *Psycholinguistics.* Boston, Massachusetts: Allyn and Bacon, Inc., 1970. An introductory text intended initially for psychologists unfamiliar with current trends in linguistics. Includes an emphasis on the transformational-generative model of language.

Fries, Charles C. *Linguistics and Reading.* New York: Holt, Rinehart and Winston, Inc., 1962, 1963. One of the first linguists to take up the issue of learning to read from a linguistic perspective, Fries provides information about the nature of the reading process, what must be learned to read satisfactorily, features of materials, and pedagogical principles involved in learning to read for a structuralist's view of language.

Lefevre, Carl. *Linguistics and the Teaching of Reading.* McGraw-Hill, 1963. Lefevre's book presents its readers with linguistic information that was held during the early sixties. For those who wish to compare and contrast current beliefs about language and reading with some earlier assumptions, this book is recommended. Lefevre's treatment of suprasegmentals is especially interesting.

Singer, Harry, and Robert B. Ruddell, eds. *Theoretical Models and Processes of Reading,* 2d ed. Newark, Delaware: International Reading Association, 1976. A collection of articles grouped into three main sections—processes, models, and issues in research and teaching—represents, broadly, the areas of opinion and research of current interest in reading and reading research. Intended, principally, to stimulate further theory formulation and research on the reading process.

The Nature of Language

Language is learned by us so early in our lives and used by us so constantly that we seldom stop to analyze the components of this communication system or how we learned its intricacies. Although language learning may be taken for granted, the importance of language cannot be overestimated. Language not only makes it possible for us to communicate with others and to preserve that communication, it also influences how we think and how we symbolize and relate to experience.

Language is the system for conveying meaning whether the meaning is transmitted in oral or written form. Reading depends upon the processing of printed language symbols to arrive at meaning in much the same way as listening depends upon the processing of acoustic language symbols. The symbolic thinking required in reading involves processing language information encoded in the written language just as the thinking required in listening involves processing the oral language code.

In this chapter we examine the nature of language by presenting definitions of language, by describing the functions of language, by noting characteristics of language, and by explaining the categories of language information that are utilized in the reading process.

Language Defined

Language is a system for sharing meaning, a framework for human communication that establishes relationships between the overt realization of language and underlying meaning. Wardhaugh defined language as "a system of arbitrary vocal symbols used for human communication."[1] Lefevre defined it in this statement, "In objective

---

[1]Ronald Wardhaugh, "The Study of Language," in Richard E. Hodges and E. Hugh Rudorf, eds., *Language and Learning to Read* (Boston: Houghton Mifflin Company, 1972), p. 14.

linguistic terms, language is a communication system patterning in objectively know-able ways within the rambling totality of the flowing stream of speech. Speech is a complex system of intricate patterns, understood in common by native speakers and native listeners."[2] Another linguist, Carroll, wrote, "A language is a socially institu-tionalized sign system."[3] In another source, Lefevre said succinctly, "A language is a system—a learned arbitrary system of vocal symbols—functioning in a specific cul-ture."[4] Hodges and Rudorf said simply that "language is the medium we use to con-vey meaning," and that "language is the framework for ideas expressed through speech and writing."[5]

These definitions stress the systematic nature of language, concentrate on the oral realization of language, and emphasize the communicative function of language. Consequently, we may define language as a coding system for meaning which lan-guage is conceived of as more than speech or writing. In this view, speech and writing are processes of communication, but language is the system through which speech and writing are given communicative functions. In speaking or writing, language is the communication system, but the system is not the same as the process.

Each language consists of a set of principles for producing and understanding ut-terances of the language thus enabling members of that language community to share meanings. This systematic patterning becomes so well learned that speakers and lis-teners are generally oblivious to the overt manifestation of the language and conscious only of the meanings.

Language Characteristics

The preceding definitions of language contained a number of terms discussed below as characteristics of language. Each of the terms—system, arbitrary, vocal, human, and communication—represents a key concept in defining language.

LANGUAGE IS UNIQUELY HUMAN

Only humans have developed language as traditionally conceptualized. Although ani-mal communication has been studied by a number of scientists, distinctions between animal communication and human communication can be made. One of these is the distinction between *emotional* and *propositional* language. Although animals may e-mit sound signals by which they express emotional states such as fear, playfulness, and anger, these sound signals appear to be involuntary and uttered instinctively only when the animal is in the emotional state that gives rise to the sound signal. Since these sound signals give direct expressions to the emotional state, the system is termed emotional "language." Propositional language, on the other hand, may designate something but not express it directly. For example, humans are able to talk about fear or anger while not actually in either emotional state. Propositional language

---

[2]Carl A. Lefevre, "Language and Self: Fulfillment or Trauma?" Part I, *Elementary English* 43 (Febru-ary, 1966):126.
[3]John B. Carroll, *Language and Thought* (Englewood Cliffs, New Jersey: Prentice-Hall, Inc., 1964), p. 8.
[4]Carl A. Lefevre, *Linguistics and the Teaching of Reading* (New York: McGraw-Hill Book Company, 1964), p. 27.
[5]Richard E. Hodges and E. Hugh Rudorf, eds., *Language and Learning to Read* (Boston: Houghton Mifflin Company, 1972), p. 5.

further differs from emotional language in that it allows for discussion of past events and speculation about the future.

Another comparison between animal communication systems and human language distinguishes the organizational structure of the system. An animal system is composed of either a small set of discrete sound signals, each of which has a specific meaning (such as a signal for danger), or is composed of sound signals that vary along a continuum (such as the bees' dance to communicate direction and distance of food). However, the sound signal for danger is always the same, and the bees' dance is always only a variation of the same message. Human language allows an infinite number of combinations of a set of discrete signals and is thus structurally vastly more complex than any animal communication system. This complex structure allows the creativity and novelty not found in animal communication systems.

LANGUAGE IS ARBITRARY AND SYMBOLIC

Language symbols are related to concepts or objects in the real world through arbitrary pairings. Words or combinations of words represent ideas or concepts, but there is no inherent connection between the word and its meaning, only a conventionalized connection.

Language symbols represent meaning, but the symbols themselves do not contain meaning. Meaning itself is contained in the speaker or listener or writer or reader, not in the symbols. The language system operates only through the conventionalized pairing of the objects or concepts and the symbols that represent those objects or concepts.

LANGUAGE IS SYSTEMATIC

Language in fact has two systems—a system of sound and a system of meaning comprised of the semantic and syntactical features of the language. In any given language the sounds of which the phonological system is composed are restricted. Only certain sounds or sound combinations are used by speakers of any language. English, French, German, and Spanish are different phonologically because the patternings of phonological signals are based upon different sets of principles.

In the same way that only certain combinations of sounds are within the phonologic system of a language, only certain combinations of words are possible in a language. Word combinations and sequences are based on the principles of syntax and semantics that are part of the particular language. Languages differ in how they signal similar relationships. For example, the process employed to show pluralization, tense change, or possession differs from language to language, but within a given language these signalling processes are systematic and constant.

THE PRIMARY FORM OF LANGUAGE IS ORAL

All human cultures have an oral language; most have both oral and written language codes; but there are primitive societies in which the language system is only oral, without a written code. This is not to say that primitive societies have an impoverished language, but rather only that the secondary, written form has not developed.

For children, learning the written code is considerably more difficult than acquiring the oral code. The secondary nature of the written code with its abstractness as a symbol system contributes to the difficulty of learning to read and write for some elementary school students.

LANGUAGE IS SPOKEN IN DIALECTS

Language is spoken in dialects which are influenced by social class, geographical regions, and the ethnic group of the speakers. Differences in language may be found in the speech of members of a distinct social class, a geographical region, or an ethnic group which characterize those speakers as different from other speakers of the same language. Dialects are simply the varieties in which language is spoken. Every speaker of English speaks a variety of the English language. The characteristics of an individual's speech have been influenced by the speech of his or her community, family, and the other models to which that individual was exposed. A speaker learns the features of the language which surrounds him or her because these features serve to promote communication. Although the social values placed on various dialects may differ, and certain dialects are more prestigious, dialects imply only differences, not a language deficiency. In written language most of the features that would distinguish one as dialectically different from another are obscured. Standard or conventionalized spelling is used in writing along with other conventions that do not reflect variations in the pronunciation of individual words or in the elisions of words even though these may be found in speech.

The Function of Language

The primary function of language is to convey meaning. Hanna, Hodges, and Hanna stated, "Every language has the ultimate purpose of enabling man to communicate information to others; it is a means by which man's personal experiences with his environment can be systematically symbolized and related to others."[6] Petty and Starkey described language as "a tool of man—essentially a tool that he uses in his thinking, in his communicative acts, in his social intercourse."[7] Shane et al. commented on the human aspect.

> Language also is the trademark that certifies us as human even as it preserves a record of our accomplishments and failures as human beings. It can be made a powerful vehicle for conveying our feelings and emotions; for expressing our hopes, illusions, fears, or wisdom."[8]

Lefevre wrote, "Language and language alone makes possible human communication, cooperation, and interaction."[9]

---

[6]Paul R. Hanna, Richard E. Hodges, and Jean S. Hanna, *Spelling: Structure and Strategies* (Boston: Houghton Mifflin Company, 1971), p. 4.

[7]Walter T. Petty and Roberta J. Starkey, "Oral Language and Personal and Social Development," *Elementary English* 43 (April, 1966):386-94.

[8]Harold G. Shane, "The Increasing Importance of Language Arts Research," in Harold G. Shane, ed., *Interpreting Language Arts Research for the Teacher* (Washington, D.C.: Association for Supervision and Curriculum, 1971), p. 1.

One sphere of living in which the enormity of language is evident is that of the world of the school. In school, language is central to all learning, and to help individuals use language well is the primary goal of language education at all levels. Shane claimed that, "Language power serves to undergird the future academic progress of children more than does any other single asset." [10] The academic progress of children is closely tied to power in one form of language: reading. Success or failure in reading has, in turn, an immense effect not only on achievement but also on attitude and self-concept.

The observation of Rosen that "schools are language-saturated institutions" [11] is an apt one. We must all acknowledge rightly or wrongly that language is the vehicle through which most teaching occurs. However, for learning to occur the learner must link the ideas expressed by the teacher and the language used in school to his personal and present conceptual, experiential, and linguistic frame of reference. Moreover, improving communication abilities must include an enriching of experience in order to foster communication. Loban interrelated the importance of language and experience: "Through experience and through language we learn. Experience needs language to give it form. Language needs experience to give it content." He elaborated further, "Learners need to be open to experience to live fully, and to arrange, shape, and clarify their experience by expressing it in effective language. Here is the base of all true education, whether in school or in all life." [12]

Catagories of Language Information

In order to communicate, language users employ the framework which is language. The framework itself consists of subsystems or categories of language information whether the language is spoken or written. In oral language these subsystems are the phonologic, the syntactic, and the semantic systems. In written language the three parallel systems are the orthographic, the syntactic, and the semantic systems.

THE PHONOLOGIC SYSTEM

In oral language not all the sounds contribute to meaning. Those that do, significant sounds, are termed phonemes—speech sounds that, when combined with other speech sounds, contribute to meaning and meaning variation. More precisely, phonemes are patterned into morphemes (meaning units), and these morphemes are in turn patterned into grammatical structures. Morphemes are the smallest meaning-bearing units of a language and may be defined as minimally significant grammatical units that contribute to the meaning of a word. Words are, in fact, single morphemes or combinations of morphemes, and the meaning of a word is dependent

---

[9] Carl A. Lefevre, "Language and Self: Fulfillment or Trauma?" Part I, *Elementary English* 43 (February, 1966):126.

[10] Harold G. Shane et al., *Improving Language Arts Instruction in the Elementary School* (Columbus, Ohio: Charles E. Merrill Publishing Company, 1962), p. 11.

[11] Harold Rosen, "Towards a Language Policy Across the Curriculum," in Barnes, Douglas, *Language, the Learner and the School* (Harmondsworth, England: Penguin Books, 1971), p. 119.

[12] Walter Loban, "What Language Reveals," in James B. McDonald, ed., *Language and Meaning* (Washington, D.C.: Association for Supervision and Curriculum Development, 1966), p. 73.

upon the morphemes of which it is comprised and (if it consists of more than a single morpheme) the order in which the morphemes occur within the word.

The combinations or patternings of phonemes into morphemes are governed by rules such that the number of phonemes combined and the order of their occurrence contribute to meaning. For example, *old* differs from *sold* in the number of phonemes present, and *bat* differs from *tab* in the order of phoneme occurrence. At the same time, these patternings of phonemes are restricted to certain combinations. For instance, *s* may be combined with *p* as in *spin* but cannot be combined with *b* as in *sbin* in English.

Not all variations in sound signal variations in meaning, nor are they all even considered separate or distinct sounds. Linguists have identified sound differences in languages which native speakers-listeners may not heed. In the words *pin, spin,* and *lip,* a native English user would not consider the *p* sound to differ, yet there are demonstrable differences. If you pronounce each word, you may note that there is a puff of air accompanying the *p* in *pin* but not in the other two words, and the *p* in *lip* differs from the other two *p* sounds in that the "sound" is not quite completely released. However, English speakers do not pay attention to these sorts of variation in sound because they do not signal meaning variation. The phoneme *p* is thus a category of speech sounds inclusive of the *p* in *pin, p* in *spin* and *p* in *lip.*

Variations in speech sounds due to such factors as dialect differences or the context surrounding a word may affect the pronunciation of a word yet not signal meaning variation. As an example of the effect of the dialect factor on speech sound variation, consider reduction of final consonant clusters such as the pronunciation of des' for desk, a feature found in many of the several varieties of Black English. This feature would not signal a meaning difference between des' and desk even though there is a distinguishable difference in the two pronunciations. Similarly, the role of context, while affecting pronunciation, may not affect meaning and thus is not a significant phonemic feature of the language. As an illustration of this, note the differences in pronunciation of *and* in *bread and butter* (bread 'n' butter), *Sally and Steve* (Sally an' Steve) and *and it happened* (and it happened) as they occur in oral language. As one can observe, there are three different pronunciations, but these differences do not affect meaning.

On the other hand, however, there are other aspects in oral language which do signal meaning variation. One of these is *juncture.* Juncture is a pause in oral language. Short but noticeable pauses between words or word parts signal differences in meaning. For example, the differences between *I scream* and *ice cream,* between *a head* and *ahead,* and between *nitrate* and *night rate* are signalled in oral language by the point where the juncture occurs. *Intonation* and *stress* are other aspects of the phonology that signal meaning differences: intonation distinguishes declarative sentences from questions; where stress is placed distinguishes *white house* from *White House.*

Each and every natural or spoken language possesses some systematic set of sound-variation–meaning-variation principles—a phonologic system. Although the system regulating the sounds and sound sequences of the language may be quite different in other languages from those found in English (in Chinese, for example, rising tone and falling tone are significant features of phonology), the phonologic system of any language serves analogously to that of English in systematically establishing relationships between sound variation and meaning variation. As language users acquire their native language, they learn the specific principles and significant features that establish the pairings between phonemes and meanings in that language. And they do so to such a level of proficiency that the attention paid to the sound variations per se occurs unconsciously. In oral language a communication occurs through the phonologic system, but the sounds themselves serve only as the code for the communication.

THE ORTHOGRAPHIC SYSTEM

The orthographic system of a language consists of visual symbols, which represent sounds, which pattern into units of meaning. These visual symbols may represent meaning logographically as in Chinese in which each symbol or character stands for a different word. Orthographic symbols may represent meaning syllabically as in Japanese in which each symbol represents a single oral syllable. Or, as in English, the visual symbols may represent individual sound segments or patterns of sounds.

Writing systems are historically secondary to oral languages and are traditionally attempts to capture the oral language sounds in a systematic fashion. By so doing, orthography provides for communication across time, across great distances, and to great numbers of people. The system employed in most modern writing is alphabetic, using graphic symbols that correspond to speech sounds. A perfect correspondence with one and only one sound represented by each graphic symbol would be a form of phonemic writing. Although there are several languages with a high degree of phonemic regularity in the orthography, English is not highly phonemically predictable. This fact has given rise to many attempts to reform English spelling so that it would be more directly phonemic. In English, phonemes may be represented in the orthography in more than one way by using letters or letter combinations (long *e* as *ee* in *peek* or *ea* as in *team*). At the same time, not all sound variation is directly represented in the orthoghaphy. The final phonemes of *books, his,* and *lunches* are all spelled the same yet pronounced differently. Similarly the final phonemes of *liked, opened,* and *hounded* are pronounced differently without variation in the orthography.

However, this lack of a perfect correspondence between speech sounds and their spelling is not all bad. For example, the use of standard spellings, though not perfectly representing speech sounds, avoids the variation in spellings which would come about due to dialect variation. Standard spellings obscure dialect differences allowing written language to be understood more widely. Also, different spellings of the same oral language sounds reduce what may be ambiguity in oral language. *Aisle* and *isle* represent the same combination of phonemes, but represent different concepts. In speech with little or no context, these may be ambiguous. In the orthography, on the other hand, spelling provides necessary clues as to which concept is meant.

The orthography also consists of special signs such as punctuation and diacritical marks. These features provide information not found directly in the phonemes of the oral language. *Aisle* and *isle* differ from *I'll* not only in spelling but also in special features of orthography. Another function that punctuation serves is to represent and signal some of the intonation patterns of oral language (e.g. *It was Tom,* and *It was Tom?*).

THE SYNTACTIC SYSTEM

Syntax is the set of principles for combining or arranging the lexical items (words) of a language in meaningful ways. Random combinations of words are not meaningful. Meaningful sentences are composed of the words of a language combined according to certain internal structural principles of word order.

In producing a sentence, a speaker begins with meaning and ends with sound. Syntax functions as a link between meaning and sound specifying the acceptable ways in which the lexical items, which represent meaning, may be combined or arranged. The sounds realized, the lexical items that these sounds represent, and the arrangement of the lexical items are directed by the speaker's intentions, but the overt manifestation has meaning in the language only if the speaker makes use of the syntactic principles of his or her language. The random sequencing of lexical items will not signal the meaning intended by the speaker. For example, *The bit man dog the* is a sequence of lexical items that has no meaning in English. But *The dog bit the man,* a sentence constructed according to the syntactic principles of English, is meaningful. However, the sentence *The man bit the dog,* due to syntactically acceptable but different ordering of lexical items, means something quite different from *The dog bit the man.* What distinguishes meaningful utterances of a language from those which are not and serves to establish the relationships between the lexical items is the syntactic system.

THE SEMANTIC SYSTEM

Language is a way of symbolizing reality by constructing categories or concepts to which experience is related. Language symbols serve, in a sense then, as labels and constructs for experience representing, in a systematic fashion, meaning as it is derived from experience.

The semantic (meaning) system of a language is comprised of these symbol-referent pairings and the selection restriction rules for the semantic components of these pairings. That is, in addition to the specific conceptual referent represented by the language symbol, each of the lexical items contains semantic components governed by selection restrictions. For nouns, for example, the semantic components include such features as concrete/abstract, masculine/feminine, common/proper and animate/inanimate. Usually a noun of the language may be concrete or abstract, masculine or feminine, etc. It is because of these semantic components and the rules (selection restrictions) governing their combinations that the "sentence" *John's typewriter slept poorly and had bad dreams* makes no sense (except metaphorically) in English. Sentences like these are semantically anomalous because the semantic components (*inanimate,* among others, for typewriter and *animate,* among others, for dreams) are incompatible.

It is important to note that language symbols—whether oral/auditory or graphic—are in themselves meaningless. Only when these symbols represent experience in the form of meaningful constructs shared by users of these symbols is meaning communicated. Listeners and readers do not "get" meaning from language symbols unless they already "have" the meaning the symbols represent or unless they are able to add or assimilate new meaning because of sufficient prior knowledge to deal with the concepts—both the lexical meaning and the semantic components—represented by the language symbols employed. Listeners who share common experiences with speakers and readers who share common experiences with writers are capable of communicating about those experiences only if they share, to a large extent, the same conventionalized pairings of symbols with experiences.

INTERRELATING THE LANGUAGE SYSTEMS

Our discussion of language subsystems as discrete systems does not imply that in language instruction these systems may be separated. In language, whether oral or written, these subsystems interrelate to provide language information through their interdependence. It is our position that only when the interrelatedness of these systems is recognized and preserved throughout instruction will growth in language-communication skills be appropriately promoted. The meanings carried by the framework (language) are derived through a simultaneous processing of the information provided by phonology, syntax, and semantics in oral language and by orthography, syntax, and semantics in written language. To make language artificial by dissecting its parts is to destroy the nature and function of language and is deleterious to growth in language-communication.

Concluding Statement

The role of language in living and learning is immense. Language is a system for the communication of meaning. To communicate in both spoken and written language, language users draw on the subsystems of language—the phonologic, the orthographic, the syntactic, and the semantic systems.

Teachers of reading need to know the nature of the language to be processed in reading and to be informed about the significance of each of the subsystems in language use and language learning. The subsystems function concurrently in the reading process, but in some teaching of reading the subsystems are distorted and taken from meaningful context. Reading for meaning requires the processing of the interrelated subsystems of language, not proficiency in recognizing small fragments of language.

Suggested Readings

Bornstein, Diane D., ed., *Readings in the Theory of Grammar,* Cambridge, Massachusetts: Winthrop Publishers, Inc., 1976. Papers addressing traditional grammar, historical grammar, descriptive grammar, transformational grammar, and language variation are collected in this book. For those interested in going beyond introductory, survey readings in grammar to original sources, this book is recommended.

Chomsky, Noam, *Syntactic Structures,* The Hague: Mouton, 1957. Chomsky's widely regarded first major work in proposing a transformational-generative model for grammar.

Chomsky, Noam, *Aspects of the Theory of Syntax,* Cambridge, Massachusetts: The M.I.T. Press, 1965. Chomsky's revisions of his earlier model include the growing influence of cognitive psychology on linguistic study and a larger role in the theory for semantic considerations.

Langacker, Ronald W., *Language and Its Structure: Some Fundamental Linguistic Concepts* (2nd Edition). New York: Harcourt, Brace Jovanovich, 1973. Drawing from structural as well as transformational-generative language theories, Langacker's book includes the major concepts of current study in linguistics in a readable form.

La Palombara, Lyda E., *An Introduction to Grammar: Traditional, Structural, Transformational.* Cambridge, Massachusetts: Winthrop Publishers, Inc., 1976. This introductory survey of language study presents three major grammar systems in the order of their development: traditional, structural, and transformational. Of note is the author's comparison of Chomsky's *Syntactic Structures* model and his later *Aspects* model.

The Language Learner

The learner of reading is a user of language and has been a language learner for years before learning to read. To learn to read a child must learn to process language presented through the medium of print. A view of reading as a language process encompasses not only the nature of language but the nature of the language learner and language learning—the learning of both the spoken and written language codes and the learning of the relationships between the two. Basing reading instruction on the existing language performance and competence of the reader requires that teachers be familiar with the language acquisition process and aware of the language each child brings to school with him.

In this chapter we examine language acquisition, the concepts of linguistic performance and linguistic competence, and the linguistically different child and also present a humanistic view of language and the language learner.

Language Acquisition

The terms *language development* and *language acquisition* are often used synonymously. However, linguists who have studied how children learn to speak their native languages refer to this process as *language acquisition* and use the term *language development* in reference to the extension and refinement of language use and language learning beyond the initial acquisition stage of the preschool years. The topic of language acquisition is discussed here because the language learning a child brings to school affects his school learning and because the acquisition of language demonstrates that children learn language, not in small piecemeal stages, not by being taught sounds, words, and sentences separately, not by being told rules, but through natural exposure in their environment and efforts to communicate. Extensive studies of language acquisition document the process of language learning. Wick Miller stated, "Language develops and unfolds very naturally and regularly seemingly according to a timetable." [1]

Although differing theories with differing degrees of emphasis on biological, cognitive, and environmental factors on language acquisition are postulated by authorities, there is a general sequence to the acquisition process. [2] In the first stage, the cooing stage, crying and gurgling sounds are produced but not the sounds of human language. At about six months the babbling stage begins. The vocal behavior of the babbling stage is still not called language, but the infant does have control over the sounds produced, and can frequently repeat certain sounds. The sounds produced at this stage are sounds found in languages, but some sounds produced are not found in the particular language an individual child hears and will learn. A baby has the capacity to learn the language of any culture, but the language environment to which he belongs determines the language he does learn.

At about the age of one year, a child starts to evidence the learning of speech by producing the first word. About six months later he can construct two-word sentences. Menyuk reported that all the basic structures used by adults to generate sentences were found in the grammar of nursery school groups. [3] Wilkinson also noted that by three-and-a-half to four a child has mastered most of the sentences found in adult speech. [4] Although these basic sentence types are evident, the language learning is far from complete since the child has much yet to master in language flexibility, complexity, and elaboration. It should be noted that, although children's sentences demonstrate gradual comprehension of the underlying structure, these sentences are not repetitions or imitations of sentences they have heard but sentences they have never heard before. Children exhibit an amazing ability to discover the systematic nature of their language and to use that system to communicate.

Jean B. Gleason commented on the sequence and extensiveness of language learning in the preschool years.

> In the year and a half that intervenes between his first two-word utterance at eighteen months and his third birthday, the child learns all the essentials of English grammar. By the age of thirty-six months many children can produce all of the major English sentence types up to about ten words in length. And by the time a child enters school, his knowledge of English is so vast and complex that no one has yet been able to program the most sophisticated computer to turn out the sentences that any five-year-old can produce with ease and assurance. [5]

The language acquisition process was described by Frank Smith as a task in which the language learner must discover the rules of grammar—uncover the structure that

---

[1] Wick Miller, "Language Acquisition and Reading," in James Walden, ed., *Oral Language and Reading* (Champaign, Illinois: National Council of Teachers of English, 1969), p. 31.

[2] Stanley Wanat, "Language Acquisition: Basic Issues," in John F. Savage, ed., *Linguistics for Teachers* (Chicago: SRA, Inc., 1973), pp. 42–47.

[3] Paula Menyuk, *Sentences Children Use* (Cambridge, Massachusetts: The MIT Press, 1969).

[4] Andrew Wilkinson, *The Foundations of Language* (London: Oxford University Press, 1971), p. 55.

[5] Jean B. Gleason, "Language Development in Early Childhood," in James Walden, ed., *Oral Language and Reading* (Champaign, Illinois: National Council of Teachers of English, 1969), p. 16.

lies beneath the surface of every utterance. It is this structure which bridges the gap between sound and meaning. Smith stated: "The child in effect performs a detection task—he hears a sentence and tries to determine a possible rule by which it could be produced."[6]

The language learner must learn the sound system, the semantics, and the syntax of his native language. The child's acquisition demonstrates the ability to discriminate and pronounce the sounds of his native language and the discovery and application of the knowledge of the rules for combining sounds into words and larger units. Of course, the child cannot state the rules, but his utterances show his internalization of the structural patterns of the language.

At the time he enters school at age five or six, a child brings considerable linguistic wealth with him. The child from an adequate, normal home environment has internalized the features of the language of his home and cultural group by the time of school entrance. In the preschool years he has accomplished an amazing intellectual task in the acquisition of his native language. He has mastered the basic sentence patterns, has learned thousands of words, and has acquired mastery of the phonology or sound system in order to produce the sounds needed for communication. Roger Brown said: "Most children, by the time they are ready to begin school, know the full contents of an introductory text in transformational grammar."[7] They have this knowledge, not in the sense of being able to verbalize such knowledge but can perform as if they possessed such knowledge.

Although the child arrives at school with a relatively sophisticated mastery of the native language, the school experiences should place heavy emphasis on continuing language development, exposure, opportunities for communication, and expanding experiential background to extend language facility since this mastery is by no means complete. Although the school beginner can communicate quite well with the oral language system, this is not enough. To be literate, he must extend his communication skills and must learn the written code.

As a user of language the child is both a language receiver and a language producer. At the time of school entrance, the child is already both a language producer and a language receiver with the oral code. However, with the written language, most children upon entrance to kindergarten and first grade have not yet learned to be language producers through writing or language receivers through reading. Figure 1 charts the language production and reception status of a child at time of school entrance.

ORAL (known)

A receiver of language——listening

A producer of language——speaking

WRITTEN (unknown)

A receiver of language——reading

A producer of language——writing

FIGURE 1. The Language Learner at Time of School Entrance

---

[6]Frank Smith, *Understanding Reading: A Psycholinguistic Analysis of Reading and Learning to Read* (New York: Holt, Rinehart and Winston, Inc., 1971), pp. 55–56.

[7]Roger Brown, "Introduction," in *Teaching the Universe of Discourse* by James Moffett (Boston: Houghton Mifflin Company, 1968), p. v.

Although parents and teachers are cognizant of the child's ignorance of written language, they may take for granted the amount of language learning the child has already accomplished, or may overlook his ability as a language learner, or may not capitalize on his linguistic capacities in teaching reading (a process that requires linguistic abilities!). The child is not new to the learning of language. However, he finds the learning of written language to be new. The existing oral language knowledge and language learning ability should be used as a base for teaching reading.

Linguistic Performance and Competence

An understanding of the language learner requires examination of the concepts of linguistic performance and linguistic competence as they are used in linguistic study and as they apply to teaching reading and communication skills. Actual observed language behavior is classified as *linguistic performance;* hypothesized judgments and knowledge that underlie that observed performance are referred to as *linguistic competence.*[8] Carroll defined competence as what is actually learned and performance as the manifestation of that learning in behavior. He elaborated:

> When the child learns his language, what is actually learned is a very complicated set of habits that can be assumed to exist as dispositions of his nervous system; these habits or dispositions are, of course, inaccessible to direct observation. The only way we can know about them, even inferentially, is through the analysis of the speaker's performance i.e., his use of them in talking or understanding, or even in reading and writing.[9]

Wardhaugh also said that linguistic performance is what a speaker or hearer actually says or hears, and that competence is the knowledge he somehow draws upon in making and understanding utterances.[10]

Goodman applied the concepts of performance and competence in building instructional theories in teaching reading and cautioned that the two concepts of what a person is capable of doing and what he is observed to do must not be confused.[11] In observing the performance of a language learner, we must not assume that all the internalized competence is observable.

In the past, teachers may have assumed that for children who did not speak freely in the school situation and for those children whose language did not reflect standard or accepted patterns that linguistic competence was lacking when in effect what they observed was only a small portion of linguistic performance. It must be remembered that children from differing social circumstances have acquired language and that they have considerable linguistic competence which teachers must seek to draw out through situations in which children exhibit linguistic performance.

---

[8]Charles Read, "Pre-school Children's Knowledge of English Phonology," *Harvard Educational Review* 41 (February, 1971):4.

[9]John B. Carroll, "Psycholinguistics and the Elementary Language Arts," in James Walden, ed., *Oral Language and Reading* (Champaign, Illinois: National Council of Teachers of English, 1969), p. 5.

[10]Ronald Wardhaugh, *Reading: A Linguistic Perspective* (New York: Harcourt, Brace and World, Inc., 1969), p. 36.

[11]Kenneth S. Goodman, "Orthography in a Theory of Reading Instruction," *Elementary English* 49 (December, 1972):1254.

Implications of Language Learning for Reading

The processes of learning to read and learning to speak are not the same. There are however certain implications to be drawn from an analysis of the process of and the setting in which spoken language is acquired which seem applicable to the teaching of the written code. In learning his language, the child does not merely repeat or imitate but learns to produce language as he *responds* to and *interacts* with his environment. Children learn language through active involvement and interaction with other language users.

As a child first learns to talk, he is positively reinforced by the significant people in his environment. He is not constantly corrected or programmed in any sequence or repetition; rather, he is constantly exposed to meaningful language as a part of the total environment. Through such exposure and through human capacity for language learning he does learn the communication system. Yet, much of the naturalness of language learning is removed from the learning of written language.

The best way to learn language seems to be to have exposure to lots of adult talk. No attempt is made to control the speech a child hears. No attempt is made to teach sounds before words. No attempt is made to teach simple sentence patterns and their rules. Studies of the acquisition of speech show that children's utterances are generally accepted and elaborated on by parents who practice language expansion. For example, the child may say in reference to himself, "Johnny fall." A typical response by the parent is "Yes, Johnny fell down on the grass." Parental responses of this nature extend the language of the child while not rejecting the child's existing linguistic performance.

In learning oral language, the child is exposed to the total flow of meaningful communication. In teaching reading, teachers can offer exposure to the natural language of meaningful communication without artificially fragmenting or limiting language. The language experience approach (see p. 89) seems particularly appropriate in this respect since it stresses reading as natural language communication and capitalizes on the relationship between speech and print while the acceptance of a child's oral language is fostered.

Lefevre pointed out the nature of trial and error in language learning. He remarked, "Children—all humans—learn by experiment—trial and error. Language learning is no exception. This native spirit of linguistic play is our greatest single natural resource for teaching children the skills of literacy." [12] In learning reading and writing children should not be discouraged from the experimentation and the trial and error learning which was so helpful in learning speech. In instructional situations, children may be afraid of making mistakes and view the feedback as correction instead of language expansion. In reading and writing, children need to try, to experiment, to use the language. However, students' fear of making errors must be recognized by the teacher as detrimental in encouraging children to use language and as detrimental to learning to read.

Moffett also emphasized the importance of feedback and response in learning and built his recommendations for language arts programs on providing situations which

---

[12]Carl A. Lefevre, "Language and Self: Fulfillment or Trauma?" Part I, *Elementary English* 43 (February, 1966):127.

will offer feedback and response. [13] Children must use language, must experiment with it, must have substantial content to communicate, must receive feedback from others to expand and alter the form and content of their thinking. Response to and response from self, peers, teachers, and parents are essential in refining the skills of communication. The feedback and response should also be a part of learning to read.

In his reading miscue research, which examined children's oral reading performance, Goodman found that when children repeated parts of a sentence or phrase such repetitions were generally for the purpose of correcting a prior error after they had gleaned more information from the print. [14] Goodman advocated letting children correct themselves and noted that the self-correcting readers read for meaning, and it is the search for meaning which results in self-correction. A point to be remembered here is that in reading instruction teachers may be reluctant to let children make mistakes and may tend to correct too frequently, thus depriving children of the opportunity to experiment, to use trial and error learning, and to discover the correct response for themselves.

Frank Smith observed that in reading "we are far more prone to talk of mistakes and errors, and far less tolerant of the child who is hypothesis testing. I think a major insight to be gained from a study of spoken language development is that we cannot expect a child to learn simply on the basis of the rules that adults try to feed to him." [15] In teaching reading we may tend to be too rule oriented often forgetting that if we attempted to teach children the rules of syntax before children talked, learning to talk could become as laborious as learning to read is for too many children.

Another characteristic of the young child's thought and speech is that it is self-oriented. Most of his language is related to his immediate world. The implication to be drawn here is that the content of reading material is made more relevant as children read about their personal concerns and experiences. In learning to read, children should see a reason for the reading activities, and teachers need to build the personal motivation by involving children in reading material that is highly motivating.

The child learned speech easily with much exposure, much encouragement, much opportunity, and much need for communication. The learning of written language can also stress much exposure, much encouragement, much opportunity, and much need for communication.

The Linguistically Different

A child who may be identified as linguistically different is one whose oral language differs sufficiently from the language used in the school so as to possibly cause interference in learning—especially in the communication skills. Although for many children the linguistic variation may not really be an obstacle to learning, some teachers view language differences as barriers. The linguistically different child must still be recognized as a user of language, and the language he uses must be accepted and

---

[13]James Moffett, *Teaching the Universe of Discourse* (Boston: Houghton Mifflin Company, 1968), pp. 188–210.

[14]Kenneth S. Goodman, "Analysis of Oral Reading Miscues: Applied Psycholinguistics," *Reading Research Quarterly* 5 (Fall, 1969):9–30.

[15]Frank Smith, "The Learner and His Language," in Richad E. Hodges and E. Hugh Rudorf, eds., *Language and Learning to Read* (Boston: Houghton Mifflin Company, 1972), p. 43.

built upon in teaching him the skills of literacy. The two most common categories of linguistically different children are those whose native language is not English and those children who speak a variety of English that is designated as nonstandard English. Both of these classifications will be discussed here.

Why should the teacher of reading be concerned with the divergent speech? That a high rate of failure and low achievement exists among groups of children who are linguistically different has been well documented. While there are many contributing factors to this underachievement, the influence of the language barrier merits consideration. In 1965 Goodman hypothesized that, "the more divergence there is between the dialect of the learner and the dialect of learning, the more difficult will be the task of learning to read." [16] On the basis of considerable further research, Goodman changed that hypothesis. In 1973, he maintained that the divergent dialect itself was not an obstacle in learning to read but that the real problem for divergent-dialect speakers was the rejection of the dialect by teachers. [17] Simons and Johnson also reported that they found no evidence for the operation of grammatical reading interference in the reading of dialect-speaking second- and third-grade black children, although they did not study nonreaders or beginners. [18] These researchers suggest that it is the teacher's handling of dialect during instruction rather than the divergent language that is the significant factor. If the language difference is acknowledged and accepted and if knowledge of this factor is applied in planning instructional strategies, the negative effect of one factor which may contribute to difficulty can be lessened.

The linguistically different child can face special problems when asked to speak and to read with language patterns which are unfamiliar to him. In recent years this problem has recieved much attention by linguists, psychologists, and educators. Recognition of reading as language processing should focus attention on the tasks facing a reader who must process language information encoded in a language system which he finds difficult to relate to his known oral language system.

It should be noted that there is a mismatch factor between spoken and written language for all children since written language is never an exact representation of the oral code. However, the difference between the two is greater for linguistically different children. It should be noted, too, that there are more similarities than differences in standard and nonstandard English, and that the similarities should be considered in the development of materials for beginning reading.

Oral language patterns which differed from the culturally valued standard English were formerly labeled as inferior or deficient or inadequate or incorrect. In recent years, as a result of the study of the sociolinguists, nonstandard language is no longer considered to be deficient language, but a different but complete and adequate language system. [19] One characteristic of all languages is that they are systematic and patterned; nonstandard language is systematic and patterned. Furthermore, non-

---

[16] Kenneth S. Goodman, "Dialect Barriers to Reading Comprehension," *Elementary English* 42 (December, 1965):853.

[17] Kenneth S. Goodman with Catherine Buck, "Dialect Barriers to Comprehension Revisited," *The Reading Teacher* 25 (October, 1973):6–12.

[18] Herbert D. Simons and Kenneth Johnson, "Black English Syntax and Reading Interference," *Research in the Teaching of English* 8 (Winter, 1974) 339–58.

[19] Joan C. Baratz, "Teaching Reading in A Negro School" in Joan C. Baratz and Roger W. Shuy, eds., *Teaching Black Children to Read* (Washington, D.C.: Center for Applied Linguistics, 1969), pp. 92–116.

standard language serves its users as a system of communication. The problem may be viewed not as one of the adequacy of the language but as a matter of values. The problem is that, since the nonstandard language is not the valued one of the cultural mainstream, the existing language learning may not be accepted by some teachers as valid for communication.

Earlier we noted that linguists have confirmed that children have mastered the basic sentence patterns of their language by the time of school entrance at age five or six. This language mastery also includes the phonology and a considerable stock of vocabulary. What sometimes seems to be ignored is that the linguistically different child has also accomplished this feat of language learning. The language deficiency theory seems to overlook the language learning of the divergent speaker.

The linguistically different child must be viewed as an adequate language learner. He must be recognized as an individual who has mastered the language of his home and cultural group at the same rate as the standard speaking child. The language learned is different, not deficient. Where possible, the oral language patterns of the learner should be the language used in the initial teaching of reading.

RECOMMENDATIONS FOR TEACHING READING TO THE NONSTANDARD SPEAKER

In teaching reading to the child who speaks nonstandard English, several recommendations are usually given.[20] Each has advantages and disadvantages. The alternatives are not necessarily mutually exclusive, although each may be strongly supported by certain authorities.

One recommendation for the linguistically different child is to teach oral standard English before teaching beginning reading. Although learning the oral code before mastering the written one can be supported since the relationship between the two is so important in beginning reading, such a recommendation has drawbacks. The nonstandard-speaking child does have sufficient oral language to begin the teaching of reading if the reading is based on the existing language. Waiting until oral standard English is taught means a delay before reading is begun, and such a delay often means failure in reading before the child has even had a chance to learn. Another reservation is that the oral standard language may not really be mastered by the nonstandard speaker in the early years of his schooling. Shuy said convincingly that ". . . speaking Standard English, however desirable it may be, is not as important as learning to read."[21] Also, we must remember that these nonstandard-speaking children do have an oral language system that communicates in their culture, and that if a teacher cares to listen and to accept the existing language, this language can communicate in the school world too.

The statement that oral standard English does not need to be taught prior to beginning reading does not mean that oral language activities are ignored in the curriculum. The teacher must give high priority to extending communication skills, provide much input in oral language, provide situations in which children are encouraged to

---

[20]Walt Wolfram, "Sociolinguistic Alternatives in Teaching Reading to Nonstandard Speakers," *Reading Research Quarterly* 6 (Fall, 1970):9–33.

[21]Roger W. Shuy, "A Linguistic Background for Developing Beginning Reading Materials for Black Children," in Joan C. Baratz and Roger W. Shuy, eds., *Teaching Black Children to Read* (Washington, D.C.: Center for Applied Linguistics, 1969), p. 118.

communicate orally, and provide models of standard English. However, reading does not have to be delayed if the instruction is related to the language children bring with them. The nonstandard-speaking child is a user of language. The teacher can use this language as a basis for a reading program. For the beginner in reading, there is sufficient oral language to start reading instruction. Expanding the oral language to include mastery of standard forms will be a concern throughout the language arts curriculum, but lack of standard usage at the beginning need not delay learning to read. Learning to read material written in standard English will also be part of the total reading program.

Another alternative for the nonstandard-speaking child is to use commercial materials written in dialect. Although these materials do attempt to provide relevant material written in the language of the children for whom they are intended, there are disadvantages. The dialect materials are not readily available in most situations, are designed for only the beginning stages of instruction, and are often objected to violently by some parents who do not realize that such materials are designed to aid in the mastery of the beginning reading skills and that the dialect feature will be discarded after the initial learning. No set of materials will fit all the children in any classroom, and it should not be assumed that all children in an inner-city school will be speakers of a divergent dialect. Research on the reading performance of divergent-dialect speakers when using dialect materials does not support the use of such materials. Simons and Johnson reported that second- and third-grade dialect-speaking black children did not read dialect texts any better than they read standard texts.[22]

Another alternative is to use the language experience approach in which children create their own materials. The teacher using the language experience approach with the linguistically different child must be alert to record the actual language and not to correct it in order to have standard syntactical patterns. The language experience approach does not require special materials but does require an accepting, encouraging teacher who realizes that reading can be taught by recording children's spoken language, thus demonstrating the relationship between the familiar oral language and the unfamiliar written language.

Still another alternative is possible. This alternative is to have children use standard materials but to permit reading of the standard materials in dialect. Like the language experience alternative, no special materials are required, but the teacher who chooses this direction must be familiar with the features of the nonstandard dialect. In the following story, "The Parable of the Goats," Goodman illustrated the difficulty of a teacher who did not recognize the dialect interference in reading.[23]

> A group of second-graders were reading in round-robin fashion. It was Jim's turn. "There was a lot of goats," he read. "There was black goats and white goats."
> His teacher smiled encouragingly. "Would you repeat that, please, Jim," she said.
> Somewhat puzzled, Jim reread: "There was a lot of goats. There was black goats and white goats."
> Still smiling, his teacher stepped to the board. In excellent manuscript, she wrote two words. "Do you see a difference in these words?" she said.

---

[22]Herbert D. Simons and Kenneth Johnson, "Black English Syntax and Reading Interference," *Research in the Teaching of English* 8 (Winter, 1974):339–58.

[23]Kenneth S. Goodman, "The Linguistics of Reading," *Elementary School Journal* (April, 1964):7.

"Yes, they have different endings," said Jim.
"Can you read these words?" the teacher asked.
"Was, were," Jim read.
"Good," said his teacher.
"This is *was,* and this is *were.* Now read again what you just read from the book."
"There was a lot of . . ." Jim began.
"No, no!" his teacher said with some annoyance. "It's *were.* 'There *were* a lot of goats.' Now, please reread."
"There were a lot of goats. There was black goats and . . ."

There are difficulties in analyzing children's oral reading performance as a language-cued process. Typically, teachers focus on vocabulary items as the ones causing difficulty to children, often ignore the effects of dialect interference, and are unaware of the syntactical clues which children are actually using.

In the preceding comments the major concern was with initial reading instruction. Although we recommend use of the existing language for reading instruction at the beginning, it should not be inferred that standard English is not part of the total curriculum. The point is that effective communication in standard English, an objective at completion of the school career, is not the focus at school entrance. A distorted view of the relative importance of standard English must not operate as a block to learning of primary reading skills.

RECOMMENDATIONS FOR TEACHING READING TO THE NON-ENGLISH SPEAKER

In the United States we pride ourselves on our efforts to provide educational opportunities for all children. However, we need to give much greater attention to the problems of teaching reading to those children whose native language is not English, just as we must give attention to accepting and acknowledging the cultural heritage children bring to school with them when that culture is different from that of the mainstream.

The child whose native language is not English can encounter difficulty in reading if sufficient attention is not given to the relationship of reading and language. In teaching reading, decisions must be made concerning the language in which reading is to be taught. One approach is to teach reading first in the native language (with instruction in oral English either along with or after the initial reading in the native language) and then to teach reading in English. Teaching in the native language makes it possible to relate the spoken and written codes, and the reader need not struggle with a language system which is difficult for him.

Venezky stated, "By teaching reading in the native language, reading instruction can begin at an earlier age than if the standard language had to be taught first; the child's cultural heritage is honored; and a most difficult task—learning to read—is undertaken in the language that the child will always be most comfortable—his own." [24] However, he cautions that the native literacy approach has not yet been proven to be superior.

Although teaching in the native language is recommended, the practicality of this alternative is questionable in many school systems where bilingual teachers are not

---

[24]Richard L. Venezky, "Non-Standard Language and Reading." *Elementary English* 47 (March, 1970):336.

available. An alternative to the teaching in the native language is to teach oral English intensively in kindergarten and first grade and then to present reading in English—bypassing the first teaching of reading in the native language. Just as with teaching oral standard English prior to beginning reading to the nonstandard speaker, this approach delays learning to read.

In working with the oral language of linguistically different children, a teacher needs to provide active learning situations requiring communication in listening and speaking. Many pictorial aids, actual experiences, language development kits, tape recorders, literature materials, and listening stations along with many communication situations can be utilized in a program to foster communication skills.

A Humanistic View of Language

A humanistic view of language accepts each individual's language as unique and of value. A humanistic view of the language learner means that each individual's language is acknowledged as a unique feature of that individuality. Just as each individual is valued, so are his language and communication valued. Teachers should reflect an attitude that conveys that the language a child brings to school is part of him and that his language is worthy of respect and acceptance just as the child himself is worthy of respect and acceptance in a society which values the individual. Teachers must accept each child's language as it is, not as the teacher might like it to be.

Dale stated his belief that "knowledge is of most worth which enhances the dignity of persons."[25] Dale commented further, "Language can make man human and humane. We learn to know our feelings and desires by crystallizing them into words."[26] Dignity of the individual and respect for his language should undergird the opportunities offered for language learning. As students experience attempts to know themselves and their world through such crystallizing through words, such searching must not be blocked through rejection of the language used in that learning.

Humane language teaching to language learners builds linguistic competence by accepting the evidenced performance, by valuing individuals' communication, and by encouraging language communication in humanistic settings.

Concluding Statement

The view that the reader is a user of language is one tenet of the linguistic foundations of reading. The language learning of the preschool years is extensive, and the school beginner comes with considerable linguistic performance and competence. The beginning reader is already a user of language, and his existing language use is a foundation upon which reading instruction is built. Just as in the acquisition of oral language, the learning of reading must provide opportunity for experimentation, for trial-and-error learning, and for feedback and response in an encouraging, motivating environment where communication is valued.

---

[25]Edgar Dale, *Building A Learning Environment* (Bloomington, Indiana: Phi Delta Kappa, Inc., 1972), p. 50.
[26]Ibid., p. 125.

Acceptance of the language the learner brings with him is essential for all children and especially so for the linguistically different. A humanistic view of language requires acceptance of a learner's individuality. A part of that individuality is his language, just as language is a part of his membership in the human community.

Suggested Readings

Baratz, Joan C., and Roger Shuy, *Teaching Black Children to Read.* Washington, D.C.: Center for Applied Linguistics, 1969. This collection of papers published during the mid- and late-1960s represents much of the thinking related to dialect interference and learning to read at that time, including a description of dialect features commonly found in varieties of Black English.

Dale, Philip S. *Language Development Structure and Function.* Hinsdale, Illinois: The Dryden Press, Inc., 1972. A detailed analysis of children's language development is presented by Dale with consideration of syntactic, semantic, and phonologic development. Theoretical positions on language learning are analyzed and the nature of the language-learning process is stressed throughout this book.

Di Vesta, Francis J. *Language, Learning and Cognitive Processes.* Monterey, California: Brooks/Cole Publishing Company, 1974. Di Vesta's assembly of research and opinion regarding language learning and cognition is both brief and readable for those unfamiliar with these topics. The book is designed primarily as a text for an undergraduate course in educational psychology for prospective teachers.

Guthrie, John T., ed. *Aspects of Reading Acquistion.* Baltimore, Maryland: Johns Hopkins University Press, 1976. Neurological, affective, and psychological/linguistic aspects of reading acquisition and a consideration of issues in teaching reading are addressed in the papers collected in this book.

Menyuk, Paula. *Sentences Children Use.* Cambridge, Massachusetts: The M.I.T. Press, 1969. Menyuk presents theoretical considerations in language acquisition and describes research on the syntactical development of children from age two to seven.

Piaget, Jean. *The Language and Thought of the Child.* New York: World Publishing Company, 1955. In this work (one of Piaget's most widely cited), Piaget presents data on child language and thought gathered through his clinical method of child observation. From this method, Piaget postulates qualitative differences between child logic and adult logic which had been seen as quantitative differences by many other psychologists.

Vygotsky, Lev Semonovich. *Thought and Language.* Cambridge, Massachusetts: The M.I.T. Press, 1962. Vygotsky's position on the relationship between thought and language, the language behavior of young children, and the use of language as a structure for analytic and logical thought are the major components of this brief, but classic, work.

4

The Relationship
between Oral and
Written Language

Spoken and written language are interrelated in a number of ways which have implications for the learning and teaching of reading. The term *relationship* is a key concept for understanding how reading is based on oral language performance and competence. The relationships are important in understanding the process of reading as the processing of language information and in understanding how the oral code is represented in written language. Linguistically based reading instruction should be consciously based on these relationships.

The relationships are examined in this chapter according to studies of achievement, according to the code relationships, and according to the process relationships. Finally, the implications of these relationships for linguistically based reading instruction are described.

The Relationship between Achievement in Oral and Written Language

Research evidence supports the correlation of achievement in oral language with achievement in written language. Loban's longitudinal study of children's language from kindergarten through grade twelve led him to conclude, "Competence in the spoken language appears to be a necessary base for competence in writing and reading." [1] In a study of the reading achievement of monolingual and bilingual children in grades one, four, and six, Braun reported, "There is substantial evidence from the

[1] Walter D. Loban, *The Language of Elementary School Children* Research Report No. 1 (Champaign, Illinois: National Council of Teachers of English, 1963), p. 88.

study to imply a positive relationship between linguistic competence and reading performance."[2] Strickland reported, "The quality of a child's speech appears closely related to the quality of his oral and silent reading." She also noted that "the more clearly the reader understands the patterning of his language, the better will be his oral reading interpretation and his silent reading comprehension."[3]

Carol Chomsky examined the relationship between rate of linguistic development and exposure to written materials as a source of complex language input. Her results showed a strong correlation between reading exposure and language development. She reported that preschoolers who had been read to frequently and primary grade children who read independently were in higher stages of linguistic development than children of the same ages who had not had extensive reading exposure.[4]

In addition to a correlation between oral and written language achievement, some researchers have identified particular factors operating in the correlation. Ruddell observed that research "strongly suggests that facility in oral expression, particularly vocabulary knowledge and an understanding of sentence structure, is basic to the development of reading comprehension skill."[5] Tatham found that, with second and fourth graders, reading comprehension was significantly related to the degree to which the reading selections resembled the oral language patterns used by the subjects.[6]

Ruddell, citing Strickland, noted, "Her study revealed that a significant relationship existed between certain structural aspects of oral language used by children and their achievement in reading."[7] In his research, Ruddell studied the effect of the similarity of oral and written patterns of language structure on reading comprehension. He concluded: "Reading comprehension is a function of the similarity of patterns of language structure in the reading material to oral patterns of language structure used by children."[8]

There is evidence to support the contention that the relative ease or difficulty with which readers can handle written language is related to the similarity of the written language to the oral language. Support for the statement that children do expect reading material to be related to the language code they have already learned comes from the research of Weber. In a study of oral reading performance of first graders, she reported that " . . . from the very beginning the [first-grade] children expected the sentences that they read to conform to the structure of the language that they already knew and that they actively used this knowledge while they read."[9] They transferred

[2]Carl Braun, "Reading Achievement of Monolingual and Bilingual Children in Relation to Selected Linguistic Variables," in Carl Braun, ed., *Language, Reading and the Communication Process* (Newark, Delaware: International Reading Association, 1971), p. 49.

[3]Ruth Strickland, "The Language of Elementary School Children: Its Relationship to the Language of Reading Textbooks and the Quality of Reading of Selected Children," *Bulletin of the School of Education, Indiana University* 38 (July, 1962):14.

[4]Carol Chomsky, "Stages in Language Development and Reading Exposure," *Harvard Educational Review* 42 (February, 1972):1–33.

[5]Robert B. Ruddell, "Oral Language and the Development of Other Language Skills," *Elementary English* 43 (May, 1966):492.

[6]Susan M. Tatham, "Reading Comprehension of Materials Written With Selected Oral Language Patterns: A Study at Grades Two and Four," *Reading Research Quarterly* 5 (Spring, 1970):402–26.

[7]Robert B. Ruddell, "The Effect of the Similarity of Oral and Written Patterns of Language Structure on Reading Comprehension," *Elementary English* 42 (April, 1965):403–10.

[8]*Ibid.*

[9]Rose-Marie Weber, "A Linguistic Analysis of First-Grade Reading Errors," *Reading Research Quarterly* 5 (Spring, 1970):450.

their capacity for handling spoken language to the reading task. Ryan and Semmel also found that what readers expect determines their responses and that correspondences between written and spoken messages seem to be based more on meaning than on auditory and visual forms. [10]

As a result of studying relationships of achievement in oral and written language, some researchers recommend that reading materials be related to children's language patterns. After a study of first grade language patterns, Strang and Hocker concluded:

> Systematically introducing the child to these basic sentence patterns in his oral language would facilitate his beginning reading development. He should also be made aware of the way in which he manipulates the structural elements within these patterns. [11]

The research of Loban and Strickland showed that the relationship between oral language and reading achievement increases from grade four through grade six. Since the demands and breadth of reading become much greater beyond the primary level, such an increase in the achievement relationship is not surprising. At the beginning level the written language learning is far below the oral language knowledge so that the beginner is usually equipped to deal with the language demands of reading unless the reading task is so meaningless as to bypass interpretation of the language. At the intermediate grade levels children may encounter problems with syntax and semantics in written language which may be beyond their customary language use.

Although it can be argued that measures of both oral and written language achievement may evaluate the same abilities, the fact remains that a high performance on oral language measures is correlated with high reading achievement. Improvement in oral language abilities may result in improvement of reading since the oral background and oral language processing adds to the ability to process information in reading.

The Relationship Between
the Oral and Written Language Codes

Both spoken and written language are vehicles for representing and conveying meaning. As was discussed in chapter 2, language is a systematic, symbolic code for meaning in which the spoken code is the primary form of language and the written code is a secondary system. The code relationships are found in the connections between the sound system, or phonology, and the writing system, or orthography. The systems can be considered parallel; they are not the same. The similarities and the differences in the codes and how the similarities and differences relate to the teaching of reading should be considered. Lefevre noted, "Learning the skills of literacy—reading and writing—requires mastery of a dual set of closely interconnected patterns which are much alike but also greatly different from each other." [12]

---

[10]Ellen B. Ryan and Melvyn I. Semmel, "Reading As A Constructive Language Process," *Reading Research Quarterly* 5 (Fall, 1969):59.

[11]Ruth Strang and Mary Elsa Hocker, "First-Grade Children's Language Patterns," *Elementary English* 42 (January, 1965):39.

[12]Carl A. Lefevre, "Language and Self: Fulfillment or Trauma?" Part I, *Elementary English* 43 (February, 1966):127.

Carroll remarked that if there is a "content" to reading, "that content is the relation between the structure of spoken messages and the system of marks or symbols used to represent the messages." He noted that this content is not discussed in textbooks on the teaching of reading and explained the importance of oral language in reading.

> The reconstruction of spoken messages from written messages depends upon the development of the speech repertory as a whole and particularly on the ability to recognize features of the spoken language system that correspond in some way with features of the writing system.[13]

Categories of language information—phonologic, orthographic, syntactic, and semantic—were identified in chapter 2 as the categories of language information to be processed. In speech, the speaker uses and the listener detects the sounds of language, associates meaning with the words, and grasps the underlying meaning through his ability to process the syntactical patterns and lexical items used. In reading, the reader does not hear the phonemes of language but, instead, sees the graphic symbols which represent the language sounds. He then associates meaning with the words and through processing the syntax grasps the underlying meaning. The beginning reader has considerable knowledge of the spoken code, but the written code can be a perplexing mystery.

One difference between the spoken and written language codes is that written language does not contain all the signals of the oral code. Written signals of capitalization and punctuation are incomplete orthographical devices for indicating the intonational features so natural in the oral code. Fries said, "If one is to read with comprehension the graphic representations of the language signals *he must learn to supply those portions of the signals which are not* in the graphic representations themselves."[14]

Another difference between oral and written language is evident in the learning of the two systems. Speech is learned easily without formal instruction, but learning of reading and writing usually requires extensive formal instruction. However, if learning written language were planned to capitalize on the existing language learning, written language could perhaps be made more meaningful and less of an incomprehensible struggle than it seems to be for some children.

Still another difference in the language codes is that written language is generally more precise and formal than most speech. Part of the lack of correspondence between the language of reading materials and the language children use is accounted for by the difference in the formality-informality factor. The naturalness of speech is often missing in written language, thus making the task of language processing to arrive at meaning difficult for those readers who are unfamiliar with the language forms used in written material.

The major significant similarity between the codes is the use of the codes for the transmission of meaning. A listener must reconstruct meaning from the spoken code, and a reader must reconstruct meaning from the written code. But language only symbolizes meaning. Meaning itself resides in the language user.

---

[13]John B. Carroll, "A Psycholinguistic Analysis of Reading Behavior," in Albert J. Harris and Edward R. Sipay, eds., *Readings on Reading Instruction* (New York: David McKay Company, Inc., 1972), p. 49.
[14]Charles C. Fries, *Linguistics and Reading* (New York: Holt, Rinehart and Winston, Inc., 1963), p. 130.

Although knowledge of code relationships is important, this alone does not explain how the codes are processed. However, the relative ease or difficulty of language processing in reading is influenced by the connection between spoken and written language. Gibson stated that we need theory-based research that will investigate *how* the correspondences between spoken and written language make contact with each other.[15] We turn now to process.

The Relationship between the Processing of Oral and Written Language

Processing language information occurs in the receptive communication acts of listening and reading and in the productive communication acts of speaking and writing. Wardhaugh defined reading as the processing of information.[16] Although Levin claimed that linguistic analyses of the relationship between spoken and written language are essential, he also emphasized that the fundamental question in reading research is, "What is the process of reading?"[17] Our concern is for comparing the relationship between information processing in reading and the information processing that occurs in listening as vocal symbols are processed. We are also concerned with comparing the information processing that occurs in the speaking and writing dimensions of communication through oral symbols in speaking and through graphic symbols in writing.

Mattingly commented that the relationship of the process of reading a language to the processes of speaking and listening to it is much more devious than formerly thought.[18] Fries gave this explanation of language processing in listening and reading:

> The process of receiving a message through 'talk' is a responding to the language signals of his native language code—language signals that make their contact with his nervous system by *sound vibrations through the ear*. The process of getting the same message (the same meanings) by "reading" is a responding to *the same set of language signals* of the same language code, but language signals that make their contact with his nervous system by *light vibrations through the eye*. The message is the same; the language code is the same; *the language signals are the same* for both "talking" and "reading". The only essential difference here is the fact that in "talk" the means of connection to the human nervous system consists of patterns of sound waves stimulating nerves in the ear, but in "reading" the means of connection to the human nervous system consists of patterns of graphic shapes stimulating nerves in the eye.[19]

---

[15]Eleanor J. Gibson, "Reading for Same Purpose: Keynote Address," in James F. Kavanagh and Ignatius G. Mattingly, eds., *Language by Ear and by Eye* (Cambridge, Massachusetts: MIT Press, 1972), p. 17.

[16]Ronald Wardhaugh, *Reading, A Linguistic Perspective* (New York: Harcourt, Brace and Jovanovich, 1970), p. 52.

[17]Harry Levin, "Reading Research: What, Why, and For Whom?" *Elementary English* 43 (February, 1966):138–47.

[18]Ignatius G. Mattingly, "Reading, the Linguistic Process, and Linguistic Awareness," in James F. Kavanagh and Ignatius G. Mattingly, eds., *Language by Ear and by Eye* (Cambridge, Mass.: MIT Press, 1972).

[19]Charles C. Fries, *Linguistics and Reading* (New York: Holt, Rinehart and Winston, Inc., 1963), p. 119.

Also, part of the difference in the processes is related to the fact that speaking and listening are primary linguistic activities, but reading is a secondary activity which relies upon the reader's awareness of these primary activities.

Two divisions of the processing of language are decoding and encoding. Decoding refers to language reception—the decoding of a message in reading and listening —while encoding refers to the expression or production of meaning with language through speaking and writing. Each of these terms is discussed here with focus on the communication processing with language.

Decoding is a popular term in the reading literature. The term has often been used in a narrow sense to mean that letter-sound relationships are used as a reader changes (decodes) the print into speech. In Chall's popular, controversial, and much cited book, *Learning to Read: The Great Debate,* approaches to beginning reading instruction were labeled as code-emphasis or meaning-emphasis approaches, and this dichotomy may have obscured the understanding of what decoding is.[20] Quite frequently, the implication is that a reader must first decode, then proceed to associate meaning with the material being read. For too long the term decoding has meant just the use of letter-sound relationships or what many have called word attack skills. The point of view of this book is that children use more than letter-sound relationships in *decoding language.* Goodman elaborated on the decoding task in an article "From Code to What?" by explaining that in decoding a child is going from code to meaning and that code and meaning cannot be separated in the process.[21] Readers decode language using graphophonic, semantic, and syntactic information simultaneously. *Language recognition skills* may be a better term for these decoding skills than *word recognition skills.*[22]

Encoding means using language symbols to express a message. The encoding task that a language user performs in speaking and writing is one of going from meaning to the representation of that meaning. This is accomplished with vocal symbols in speaking and through graphic symbols in writing. Encoding meaning by use of the language code is the task of both a speaker and a writer. The encoding process goes from thought to language; in reading and listening the process is decoding—that is, going from the code for meaning to meaning.

In processing both print and speech, a language user (whether a listener or a reader) must determine the underlying deep structure—the representation of meaning. What the listener hears is the surface structure, just as what a reader sees on the page is the surface structure. In arriving at the deep structure it is the syntax that serves as the bridge to meaning. (See page 69.)

Relationships between Oral and Written Language: Implications for Teaching Reading

There are implications for teaching reading to be drawn from the preceding discussion of the correlation between oral language development and achievement in written

---

[20]Jeanne B. Chall, *Learning to Read: The Great Debate* (New York: McGraw Hill, 1967).

[21]Kenneth S. Goodman, "From Code to What? *"Journal of Reading* 14 (April, 1971):455–62, 498.

[22]MaryAnne Hall, "Teaching Language Recognition Skills in the Language Experience Approach," Paper presented at the International Reading Association Conference, Atlantic City, New Jersey, 1971.

language (especially reading achievement), from the discussion of the similarities between the oral code and the written code, and from the discussion of the language processing tasks involved in producing or receiving language messages. The implications for teaching reading related to the process cannot, in our judgment, be separated from the implications that are related to the nature of the written language code. Although the language codes and language processing can be separated for purposes of discussion, a false dichotomy may develop if the code and the process are not considered simultaneously in instruction.

When reading is viewed as a language processing task, attention must be given to the language abilities needed for successful reading. Carroll discussed these language abilities in some detail, and the points ennumerated below are some of those he identified.[23]

1. "The child must know the language that he is going to learn to read. Since in reading a child must be able to reconstruct messages from print that are similar to messages he can already understand in spoken form, knowledge of the spoken language is required." Although children such as the deaf or the foreign born may learn reading without first acquiring mastery of the oral language represented in the reading materials, reading instruction necessitates special adaptations when the oral foundation is lacking.

2. "The child must learn the left-to-right principle by which words are spelled and put in order in continuous text."

3. "The child must learn that there are patterns of highly probable correspondence between letters and sounds, and he must learn those patterns of correspondence that will help him to recognize words that he already knows in his spoken language or that will help him to determine the pronounciation of unfamiliar words."

4. "The child must learn to recognize printed words from whatever cues he can use—their total configuration, the letters composing them, by the sounds represented by those letters, and/or the meanings suggested by the context."

5. "The child must learn that printed words are signals of spoken words and that they have meaning analogous to those of spoken words. While 'decoding' a printed message into its spoken equivalent, the child must be able to apprehend the meaning of the total message in the same way that he would apprehend the meaning of the corresponding spoken message."

6. "The child must learn to reason and think about what he reads, within the limit of his talents and experience."

Carroll observed that the order for teaching these abilities is disagreed upon by educators but notes that most authorities agree that all of them are important. The importance of the language base is unmistakable in the above listing.

Although the relationship between oral language facility and reading achievement has been given much attention in the literature on reading and has been documented by research investigations, less attention has been given to the nature or reading problems as language problems. Difficulty in reading can be examined according to

---

[23]John B. Carroll, "The Nature of the Reading Process," in Eloise O. Calkins, ed., *Reading Forum,* (Bethesda, Maryland: National Institute of Neurological Diseases and Stroke, 1971), pp. 5–8.

ability to or difficulty in performing the language processing tasks of reading. Kagan commented on the importance of language competence in relation to understanding poor reading:

> Some of the most reliable characteristics of poor readers are their poor vocabulary, inadequate language comprehension, and faulty memory for language categories. But poor readers do not always differ from the reading competent child on non-verbal skills. Reading is characteristically facilitated by the possession of language structures which allow the child to assimilate verbal material. Thus, the association between inadequate language mastery and reading deficiency is theoretically reasonable."[24]

Other than consideration of the language mismatching present for the linguistically different child, language factors relating to poor reading performance may not have been given enough weight in relationship to reading performance.

The point made so emphatically by Lefevre that the basic fault in poor reading is lack of sentence sense may be noted here in regard to the language processing nature of reading.[25] Exploring the language processing nature of reading offers promise for analysis of the factors contributing to reading difficulties. Subsequently, lessons may be developed which focus on the language processing aspect of reading difficulties. For example, teaching strategies may be developed to focus on sentence sense and understanding meaning. In some cases these lessons may begin with developing sentence sense and meaning in oral language before proceeding to parallel instruction in the written language of reading. The key, however, is to provide the language learner with relevant and meaningful communication situations in which the potential for development of sentence sense and understanding meaning is enhanced and to help the learner grasp the concept that the written language represents meaning.

In yet another way, there are implications stemming from the relationship between the language code and language processing and achievement suggested in the previous discussion. These are drawn from the notion that language processing results in meaning. For prereaders and beginning readers emphasis should be placed upon helping them develop an understanding that the purpose of the written code is the same as the purpose of the oral code—communication. In this regard, the language experience approach to reading seems to have particular justification. As Stauffer said, "Reading is one facet of language and one means of communication and should from the very beginning be taught as such through a language-experience approach."[26] When reading is first taught by recording in writing children's oral language descriptions of experiences, these recordings contain the thoughts and language with which children are familiar and which, in turn, can promote an understanding of the concept of reading.

Preschool children have learned to be both producers and receivers of language in its oral form, and they are able to participate in many communication situations as listeners or speakers. If communication in written language builds upon the already

---

[24]Jerome Kagan, "Dyslexia and Its Remediation," in Eloise O. Calkins, ed., *Reading Forum*, (Bethesda, Maryland: National Institute of Neurological Diseases and Stroke, 1971), pp. 55–56.

[25]Carl A. Lefevre, *Linguistics and the Teaching of Reading* (New York: McGraw-Hill Book Company, 1964), p. 5.

[26]Russell G. Stauffer, "Certain Convictions about Reading Instruction," *Elementary English* 46 (January, 1969):87.

isting language and experience of the beginning reader, the potential for difficulty reduced because the concept of written language as communication is fostered. And since the written language originated from within the child, it represents his experience and is, therefore, meaningful.

Our previous discussion also suggests that an analysis of the relationships between code forms—oral and written codes—yields implications for teaching language concepts. It is strange that while many teachers sometimes seem unaware of the immense language competence of children, they take for granted that children understand the concepts conveyed by terminology such as a *letter, word, sound,* and *sentence.* These concepts of language are so obvious to adults that they are unaware that these are often concepts children of five or six do not readily understand. Downing found that five or six year olds were unable to define terms such as *word, phrase, sentence, letter,* and *sound.*[27] Since these terms are used instructionally, it would seem appropriate to help children learn the concepts represented by the terminology. This may be accomplished in prereading or beginning reading instruction through arranging functional settings in which the concepts and terminology are demonstrated. For example, teaching the concepts for which the terminology stands can be accomplished through many natural references to the terms as students match words, letters, phrases, and sentences to similar items on experience charts and through other language experience activities in using language.

Another implication for instruction suggested by the relationship between process and code is to integrate reading and writing instruction. The National First Grade Studies show that a writing component added to a regular reading program enhances achievement in reading.[28] In reading and in writing an individual is involved in different processes, although both are language-based. Reading involves *recognition* of printed symbols, and writing requires *reproduction.* Recognition is easier than reproduction as attested by studies of elementary school students' reading and spelling vocabularies which reveal that children can recognize many more words than they can reproduce. Although it is generally assumed that learning to write occurs after learning to read, there is some evidence that some young children learn to write before learning to read. Durkin suggests that there might be something "natural" about the home situation in which young children learned to read. She noted that for some early readers their ability to read was, at least in part, a by-product of ability in writing and spelling.[29] In investigations of the "spontaneous spelling" of preschool children, Read found that writing began before learning to read and that in some cases writing began as early as three-and-one-half.[30] Hall, Moretz, and Statom found in a study of early writers (three-, four-, and five-year-olds) that learning to write usually occurred before learning to read.[31] All early writers came from homes where they had observed writing by parents and siblings and where writing materials were available. Instructionally

[27]John Downing, "How Children Think about Reading," *The Reading Teacher* 23 (December, 1969): 217–30.

[28]Robert Dykstra, "Summary of the Second-Grade Phase of the Cooperative Research Program in Primary Reading Instruction," *Reading Research Quarterly* 4 (Fall, 1968):65–66.

[29]Dolores Durkin, "A Language Arts Program for Pre-first-grade Children: Two-year Achievement Report," *Reading Research Quarterly* V (Summer, 1970):537–38.

[30]Charles Read, "Pre-School Childrens' Knowledge of English Phonology," *Harvard Educational Review* 41 (February, 1971):1–34.

[31]MaryAnne Hall, Sara Moretz, and Jodellano Statom, "Children Who Write Early: An Investigation of Early Writing," *Language Arts* 53 (May, 1976):582–85.

then, early exposure to writing in preschool settings or emphasis on integrati
reading and writing may develop an awareness of and interest in the written languag
code in natural, functional situations, and can in turn enhance understanding o
these reciprocal processes.

Considerations in the development of, selection of, and use of materials for reading
instruction are also implied by relationships between the oral and written language
codes. Instructional materials for reading should be comprehensible to the readers
who will read them. The degree of potential meaningfulness as well as the similarity
between the language patterns used in the child's oral language environment and the
materials used instructionally should be examined. Where a mismatch between the
written language patterns appearing in the reading materials and the oral language
patterns of the children who are required to read these materials exists, difficulty may
occur unless teachers take steps to reduce the degree of mismatch or unless they focus
on the childrens' language processing attempts in a positive way.

Basal materials written since about 1970 are generally much improved in their
attempts to reflect the environments, values, and circumstances of social classes or
sub-cultures other than white, middle-class, male-dominated suburbia. These newer
materials also reflect an effort to include more natural language (rather then the stilted
language of earlier materials) and more relevant content than the language and content so vehemently denounced as ridiculous for the disadvantaged or insulting in their
simplicity for most children.

A further implication drawn from the relationship between the language code and
the processing of language suggests that instructional time and suitable reading
materials be made available to children so that they may have opportunity to make
use of the language processing strategies they are learning. Classrooms should
contain a wide variety of books, magazines, and other printed material for children.
Communication between the school librarian and classroom teachers can lead to the
placing of appropriate literature in the classroom. Then, instructional time should be
arranged to provide opportunity to children to read the now-available literature.

A final implication of the relationship between achievement in oral and written
language is that continuous fostering of communication abilities in oral language
should be a major curriculum concern. Too often instruction in reading is separated
from instruction in the other language arts. Even teachers who are conscientious
about providing language arts experiences may be unaware of ways in which to
strengthen learning to read through related language activities. One way to accom-
plish this is to arrange situations in which children are provided the opportunity to
play with language—manipulating, arranging, and rearranging language patterns
both orally and in written form. Also, oral familiarity with syntactic patterns and
content facilitates processing these patterns and content in reading, thus reading to
children to broaden their awareness of language patterns and story content used in
literature is recommended.

Concluding Statement

As noted earlier, research confirms that achievement in oral language and achievement in reading are correlated. However, although the relationship in achievement in

oral language and reading has been substantiated, additional research is needed to determine the effect on achievement when children are taught to maximize the clues for processing language by drawing on the relationships of the oral and written codes.

Nevertheless, the current status of research and linguistic theory yields many instructional implications that should, in our opinion, be implemented. The relationship between the oral and written codes and the similarities and differences in the language-processing tasks of reading, writing, listening, and speaking should be recognized in language arts instruction. Providing appropriate reading instruction requires a sound linguistic base from which specific reading instruction activities can be developed. Failure to pay heed to accurate and appropriate linguistic information is inexcusable.

Suggested Readings

Chomsky, Carol. "Stages in Language Development and Reading Exposure," *Harvard Educational Review* 42 (February, 1972):1–33. Chomsky's research investigates the effect of reading to children and independent reading by children on children's language development.

Goodman, Kenneth S. and James T. Fleming, eds. *Psycholinguistics and the Teaching of Reading.* Newark, Delaware: International Reading Association, 1969. This collection of papers, which explore the psycholinguistic nature of the reading process, highlights the complex relationships of oral and written language.

Hodges, Richard E. and E. Hugh Rudorf, eds. *Language and Learning to Read.* Boston: Houghton Mifflin Company, 1972. This collection of sixteen papers by known authorities in linguistics, reading, and language arts stresses the relationships between oral and written language as well as the significance of the relationships for teaching communication.

Loban, Walter. *Language Development: Kindergarten through Grade 12.* Urbana, Illinois: National Council of Teachers of English, 1976. Loban's research traces the language development of children from kindergarten through grade 12. He reports on the relationships between language development and school achievement.

Read, Charles, *Children's Categorization of Speech Sounds in English.* Urbana, Illinois: National Council of Teachers of English, 1976. Read presents psycholinguistic and pedagogical conclusions based upon his research of children's categorization of speech sounds as they attempt to spell the sounds of English.

Smith, E. Brooks, Kenneth Goodman, and Robert Meredith. *Language and Thinking in the Elementary School.* New York: Holt, Rinehart and Winston, 1976. A "language-thought-centered" view of learning and teaching is the focus of this book. The discussion of reading as a psycholinguistic process shows the relationship of oral and written language.

5

Phonology Orthography, and Language Processing

Knowledge of the relationships between the phonology, or sound system, of the language and the orthography, or writing system, should be a part of teachers' linguistic informational background. Teachers of reading, writing, and spelling should base decisions about content and teaching strategies on an accurate linguistic base. Unfortunately, the phonologic and orthographic bases of language have been frequently misunderstood in past applications to teaching reading, and some activities planned for children have been inappropriate.

In this chapter we examine features of the orthography and phonology of English and their interrelationships along with a discussion of guidelines for instruction which are derived from this examination. Although the preceding chapter dealt with an overview of the relationships between oral and written language, this chapter deals specifically with phonologic and orthographic information. However, we wish to stress that such information should not be separated from the other language systems of semantics and syntax in the teaching of reading and writing. In teaching both reading and writing, the important consideration is integrating processing with the code to provide readers with strategies for making use of the code system thus enabling them to extract meaning from the written code in a fashion which parallels extracting meaning from the oral code.

Tying Phonology and Orthography Together

When reading is built on a linguistic foundation, the nature of the relationship between the phonology of the oral code and the orthography of the written language code is one cornerstone. The nature of language as a symbol system is particularly significant in the study of phonology and orthography. The symbolization of meaning through sound and through print is the base for study of these symbol systems of language.

Even though written language is a secondary form of language, its purpose is communication just as the purpose of oral language is communication. Both language forms are codes for meaning. Yet, the teaching of written language—and particularly, the teaching of graphophonic information—has often been divorced from consideration of language processing as communication. Some of the distortion in teaching written language—especially the teaching of sound-letter correspondences in isolation—has occurred because of inadequate information about the phenology and orthography of language and a tendency to oversimplify the relationship between the two codes. Distortion has also occurred because teaching graphophonic information has often been a drill-oriented situation in which consideration of language as a code for meaning has been ignored. Meaning is the essential outcome of any language processing activity, and teaching sound-letter relationships should not divert attention from meaning.

Although we will discuss relationships between phonology and orthography, we wish to avoid the impression that the systems are identical. Although the phonologic and orthographic features of language are separate language systems, we are integrating the discussion of them because in learning to read and to write the learner draws upon his existing oral language (including tacit knowledge of phonologic principles) and because graphophonic information is both phonological and orthographical.

In the past, the nature of the orthography was not given sufficient attention in discussions of teaching phonics. In processing the written language code, the term *phonics* usually referred to teaching certain letters or letter combinations in the writing system which correspond to oral language sounds. However, proficient reading does not occur by building up to meaning through either an analysis or a synthesis of words into the sounds represented by various letters or letter combinations apart from use of other language information (syntax and semantics). Since the orthographic system of any language contains syntactic and semantic information, discussions of sound-letter correspondences that do not include a discussion of the nature of the orthographic system are incomplete. In some cases such discussions have led to a rather narrow view of graphophonic information and, consequently, some rather inappropriate content. Talking about phonics in reading apart from discussing orthographic representations seems ludicrous. How can a teacher talk about sounds in reading instruction without reference to the printed representation of the sounds since in learning to read children must learn to process written symbols? In learning the written code children need to learn the orthographic patterns for the representation of oral language patterns.

The correlation between speech and print can be overemphasized, especially in discussions of the phoneme-grapheme relationships and in the degree of emphasis placed on these relationships in beginning reading. Much has been said in reading instruction about the teaching of sound-letter or phoneme-grapheme relationships. However, simplification of the relationship between features of the phonology and orthography has led to the misunderstanding that only learning sound-letter correspondences is involved in teaching processing of graphophonic information.

The need for teachers to have an understanding of graphophonic information was well stated by Wardhaugh.

> " . . . teachers must have available to them an adequate theory of reading based on a defensible statement about the phonological structure of English. They also need a statement about how that phonological structure is related to English orthography. Any reading pedagogy without these can hardly be adequate." [1]

It is in the area of graphophonic information that linguists first had an impact on reading instruction. The early linguistic reading programs stressed a narrow interpretation of decoding with the stress on learning phoneme-grapheme relationships. Unfortunately this emphasis was usually isolated from meaning. The linguistic patterning idea may have been an improvement over the sort of hit-or-miss phonics offered in some basal programs, but children who received the linguistic instruction usually did not receive a well-rounded reading program. Also, children in other reading programs often received inappropriate content in their phonics learning.

Groff (who is an advocate of a revised and accurate sort of phonics instruction integrated with other language information) wrote, "It is axiomatic, then, that phonics (that knowledge of the certain sound-spelling relationships a child can learn to use as he masters reading and spelling), to be taught to properly function, must be based on sound evidence and/or logical thinking." [2]

Graphophonic Terminology

One identifiable influence of linguistics on reading is the use of linguistic terminology in the reading literature and in recent instructional materials. Hopefully, increased attention to accurate linguistic terms will reflect greater linguistic knowledge on the part of teachers, and not simply a new set of terms. In studying the nature of language, the reading teacher must understand the concepts inherent in the phonologic and orthographic terms.

Phonics is a term familiar to reading teachers, to parents, to salespersons of reading materials, and to all critics of current reading instruction. Generally, phonics refers to the learning of letter-sound relationships in reading; thus, phonics is the application of phonology to reading.

The terms *phonetics* and *phonemics* are sometimes used interchangeably, but these words are not synonymous. Their meanings and the distinctions between them need clarification. Both terms refer to branches of linguistic study. Phonetics—the study of speech sounds and speech production—encompasses the study of the sounds of all human language. Phonemics is concerned with the sounds of a *particular* language and how sound variations in a particular language function to convey differences in

---

[1] Ronald Wardhaugh, *Reading: A Linguistic Perspective* (New York: Harcourt, Brace and World, 1969), p. 118.
[2] Patrick Groff, "Fifteen Flaws of Phonics," *Elementary English* 50 (Jan., 1973):35.

meaning. In discussions of reading instruction, the term *phonetic analysis* is often used to describe the process of determining the sounds represented by letter units. The process is more accurately termed *phonemic* analysis since it deals with the sounds of a particular language.

The minimal units of sound are phonemes. Although technically there are differences within phonemes (such as the difference in the first sound produced when the word *pig* is spoken and the last sound produced in the spoken word *stop*), the phoneme is the minimal unit that signals a difference between words; thus a difference in meaning results. For example, the difference in the pronunciation of *cat* and *bat,* the difference in initial phonemes reflects a difference in meaning (see page 16.)

The term *grapheme* is a writing unit although it is not synonymous with *letter.* For example, in both the words *chat* and *cat* there are three graphemes. The *c* in *cat* represents one phoneme in spoken language, but in the word *chat* the first grapheme, *ch,* represents a single phoneme even though it is composed of two letters. In the word *came* there are four graphemes, although the *e* does not relate directly to a sound correspondence. It is there as a marker to provide information about other sound-letter representations in the word.

Some terms used in reading programs have changed to reflect more accurate linguistic information. For example, before 1960, it was more common to use the term *sound-letter relationships* than the term *phoneme-grapheme relationships.* Also, the term *consonant cluster* is now preferred to the designation *consonant blend* since linguists note that the blending of consonants is no more a blending of phonemes than is the combining of adjacent consonants and vowels in a word. For example, the letters *bl* in *blue* do not represent a blending of phonemes any more than does the meshing of the *bl* with the last phoneme of the word *blue.* Linguists question the terms *long* and *short vowels* since the implied connotation of duration is inaccurate and misleading. The *long vowel* is now called a *glided vowel,* and the *short vowel* is called the *unglided vowel.*

Two other terms used in relating the orthographic and phonologic systems are *markers* and *relational units.* Venezky identified markers as those written symbols which mark or give a clue to the pronunciation of certain other elements within a word.[3] For example, the *e* in *lake* is considered a marker since the *e* does not in this instance relate to a phoneme but signifies instead the sound representation of another element within the word. The *e* in *chance* is a marker for the sound represented by the second *c,* whereas the *e* in *give* is used since no English words end in *v.* Yet, in phonics instruction, all these are commonly treated as examples of "silent *e*" even though linguistically the *e* marker works in conjunction with other patterns. A relational unit in language refers to a written unit which symbolizes a relationship to sound. Thus, in the word *lake* cited above the *l, a,* and *k,* are relational units.

In addition to the terminology associated with phoneme and grapheme units, there is terminology which relates to another unit of language, morphemes. A morpheme is the minimal unit of meaning in language. Two classes of morphemes, free and bound, are included in morphological analysis. A *free morpheme* is a unit that by itself signifies meaning; a *bound morpheme* cannot function independently without other morphemic units. For example, *look* is a free morpheme, but in *looking, looks,*

[3]Richard L. Venezky, "English Orthography: Its Graphical Structure and Its Relation to Sound," *Reading Research Quarterly* 2 (Spring, 1967):85–88.

and *looked,* the *ing, s, ed* are examples of bound morphemes which are important language signals but which cannot appear separately. What is usually called *structural analysis* (analyzing word forms for meaningful word parts such as bases, prefixes, suffixes, compound words, and contractions) is probably better called *morphological analysis* since the focus is on morphemes. Morphological analysis related to the word function requires meaningful context to provide syntactical clues and to signal the word form and function with the context.

Morphophonemic is a term used by Venezky[4] to describe the nature of the English spelling system. For example, in words such as *sane* and *sanity* or *nation* and *national* the morphemic base for spelling is evident. English orthography is related to morphemic units as well as to phonemic units and spelling cannot be considered only from a phoneme-grapheme base. C. Chomsky presented a detailed analysis of examples that illustrate the morphemic base for spelling.[5] The function of morphemes in graphophonic information has been neglected, yet the morphemic considerations are particularly important in the representation of the sound system through the use of the writing system especially when a word contains more than a single morpheme.

Although teachers should be informed about this terminology and aware of these concepts, we are not recommending that the terminology be emphasized with children. However, in cases where such terms are used in instruction to children, teachers should use the most accurate terminology or employ the terminology used for instruction in the commercial materials in order to avoid the confusion that may occur if a teacher uses one term while the materials use another. Confusion may also occur if there is a lack of consistency from grade level to grade level. Thus, not only must the content of the instruction in graphophonic information be appropriate and accurate, it must also be consistent in the terminology employed.

The English Phonologic and Orthographic Systems

The phonologic system of a language identifies the sounds in that language and restricts the arrangements or combinations of these sounds. Combinations of sounds are related to meaning and variations in the combinations of sounds function to signal meaning differences in oral language.

According to Trager and Smith the inventory of English phonemes is forty-five in number.[6] This inventory includes the segmental phonemes as well as features of pitch, stress, and juncture. Although another language may include certain of the same phonemes, English as any other language is composed of a unique set. For example, although both English and Spanish include the phoneme for *a* as in *father,* English phonology does not contain the trilled *r* of Spanish. Similar comparisons can be made for other languages. We can illustrate restrictions on the combinations of phonemes by considering position constraints. For example, in English, the arrangement of phonemes in the final segments of *long* and *sing* is possible, but this combination is never found in the initial segment of an English word.

---

[4]*Ibid.*

[5]Carol Chomsky, "Reading, Writing, and Phonology," *Harvard Educational Review* 40 (May, 1970).

[6]George L. Trager and Henry Lee Smith, "An Outline of English Structure" *Studies in Linguistics: Occasional Papers No. 3* (Norman, Oklahoma: Battenburg Press, 1951, reprinted American Council of Learned Societies, Washington, D.C., 1957).

Pitch, stress, and juncture, called nonsegmentals or suprasegmentals by linguists, are also features of the phonologic system. Pitch refers to the rising or falling of speech sounds, stress to the emphasized or accented words or word parts and juncture to the separations or breaks between words or word parts. These intonation features provide information which native language users employ in processing oral language. Pitch, stress, and juncture, are not unrelated to syntactic or semantic considerations. Rather the intonation features of any oral language utterance are reflections of the syntactic and semantic systems of that language.

The orthography of English is a complex system of patterned relationships. In understanding how orthography works, one must recognize the writing system as having lexical, morphologic, and syntactic bases as well as a phonologic base. Although both the oral and written language codes represent the phonology, vocabulary, and grammar of a language, the writing system is not a perfect representation of the oral code. Gudschinsky defined a writing system as a means of visual communication analogous to, but not identical with, the system of oral communication on which it is based.[7]

English orthography is alphabetic. Frank Smith described the alphabetic principles as "the system that relates the written and spoken forms of our language through correspondences between the phonology of the one and the orthography of the other."[8] In the past, the tendency to both oversimplify and exaggerate the importance of the sound-letter relationships of language may have stemmed from a view that English orthography directly represents English phonology. Hodges elaborated, "Orthographies can be classified as simple or complex. Simple orthographies are characterized by a strict correspondence between speech and writing at some particular level of language."[9] Such strict correspondence could be on a morphemic level as in Chinese with its ideographic orthography or on a phonemic level as in Russian. Complex orthographies can be distinguished from simple orthographies because they represent language at several levels simultaneously. English is a complex orthography since it represents not only phonemic, but also morphophonemic, syntactic, and etymological features simultaneously.

Gudschinsky studied the writing systems of a number of languages. She noted that the English writing system represents phonology, lexicon (vocabulary) and grammar at various levels. Each of these linguistic systems is represented incompletely and in complex interrelationships. She explained:

> An alphabetic writing system is traditionally assumed to be a more or less regular graphic representation of the phonemes of a language, with perhaps some special spellings to represent morphophonemic data. Actually, any orthography, and especially the English system, is much more than that. At every level, the lexical and grammatical hierarchies are represented, as well as the phonology.[10]

---

[7]Sarah C. Gudschinsky, "The Nature of the Writing System: Pedagogical Implications, in Richard E. Hodges and E. Hugh Rudorf, eds., *Language and Learning to Read,* (Boston: Houghton-Mifflin, 1972), p. 100.

[8]Frank Smith, "Phonology and Orthography: Reading and Writing," *Elementary English* 49 (Nov., 1972):1075.

[9]Richard E. Hodges, "Theoretical Framewords of English Orthography," *Elementary English* 49 (Nov., 1972):1093.

[10]Sarah C. Gudschinsky, "The Nature of the Writing System: Pedagogical Implications," in Richard E. Hodges and E. Hugh Rudorf, eds., *Language and Learning to Read,* (Boston: Houghton-Mifflin Co., 1972), p. 101.

Thus, although the alphabet may be the easiest part of the language system to teach systematically, the relationships between sound and print recorded with letter symbols are more complex than many people realize.

Statements such as "English is unphonetic" or "English spelling is chaotic or unsystematic" reveal a lack of linguistic knowledge. All natural languages are phonetic because they have a system of sounds. What people generally mean by this type of unsophisticated statement is that the sound-letter relationship is not one of a precise, simple, and completely predictable one-to-one correspondence between sound and graphic symbol. However, the impression many people have that the English writing system is highly irregular is not supported by linguistic research and is an impression not held by linguists. The Stanford study of phoneme-grapheme relationships in 17,000 words found that English orthography is actually a far more consistent reflection of spoken language than had been assumed.[11] Writing in 1970, Venezky stated:

> A theoretical basis for English orthography has been established through extensive research over the past ten years. Most important to this work is the view that English spelling is not simply a defective-phonemic system for transcribing speech, but instead a more complex and more regular set of patterns in which both phonemic and morphemic elements share leading roles.[12]

The complexity of English leads some linguists to conclude, as did Chomsky and Halle in *The Sound Pattern of English*, that ". . . English orthography, despite its often cited inconsistencies comes remarkably close to being an optimal orthographic system for English."[13]

Unfortunately, the complexity of English may be a disadvantage for the beginning reader especially when considerable emphasis is placed on phoneme-grapheme relationships. We believe, however, that when reading is taught as language processing, sound-letter correspondences will be recognized as only a partial source of language information.

Although the complex English writing system is more systematic and consistent than is commonly assumed, it must be recognized that some features of its phonology and orthography do pose special problems in learning the code. One spelling problem encountered is that of the homonyms which have the same pronunciation but different spellings. Phonological information will not help to distinguish between the spelling of two different words with the same pronunciation. In such a case the syntactic or semantic level of language must be the significant cue. For elementary children it is probably easier to recognize the word form in reading than to decide which word form to spell when writing. Contextual clues in reading help the reader supply the correct meaning, but in spelling a child must rely on memory of the form associated with a particular meaning.

Another problem exists because there are only twenty-six letter symbols in the English alphabet but over forty phonemes in English. Consequently, some beginners

---

[11]Richard E. Hodges and E. Hugh Rudorf, "Linguistic Clues in Teaching Spelling," *Elementary English* 42 (May, 1965).

[12]Richard L. Venezky, "Linguistics and Spelling," in Albert H. Marckwardt, ed., *Linguistics in School Programs*, 69th Yearbook, Part II, National Society for the Study of Education (Chicago: University of Chicago Press, 1970), pp. 264–74.

[13]Noam Chomsky and Morris Halle, *The Sound Pattern of English* (New York: Harper and Row, 1968).

may be confused by the realization that some sounds can be represented a number of ways in print. For example, what is commonly called the long (glided) *a* sound can be represented by *ay* in *day, ai* in *rain, a* in *cake,* or *ei* in *eight.*

Still another problem is that a grapheme can be used to represent more than one sound. We can again use the letter *a* to illustrate the point. *A* can represent the sound heard in the middle of *hat* as well as the sound heard in the word *age.* When *a* is followed by *r,* the sound is different from either the glided or unglided *a. A* can also represent some other phonemes (*saw, father*). This problem is often over emphasized without examining position pattern clues or semantic clues which help the reader and writer.

One inadequacy of a phonemic writing system is the fact that the written language system does not reflect changes in speech forms. All language changes over time but oral language changes in more ways and changes more quickly than does written language. Phonemic writing systems are not representative of differing pronunciations of individuals and groups from various geographic regions, and words written in a standard spelling system may still have differing pronunciations from area to area. Although standard spelling is useful to writers regardless of their individual pronunciations, the spelling system does not reflect individual dialect variations. It is quite common for particular words to sound differently when they are pronounced by a native resident of Georgia, a native of Wisconsin, or one from Maine. Yet, some discussions of phoneme-grapheme relationships would give the impression that there is a standard pronunciation. What the individual learning to read needs to learn are the graphic counterparts for words already known semantically and syntactically in their oral forms. Reading may become confusing if the explanations of pronunciations of sound-letter correspondences do not match pronunciations found in natural language.

Graphophonic Information: Guidelines for Instruction

The goal of all reading instruction is to equip children with strategies for extracting meaning from print. Teaching children to employ graphophonic information as a means toward that end is one aspect of reading instruction. The intent here is to highlight this aspect of reading *in connection with* a linguistically founded reading program.

As descriptions of the linguistic theory related to orthography and phonology have increased in recent years, both linguists and educators have begun to state implications of the sound and writing systems for the teaching of written language skills. Goodman aptly noted, "Orthography must be considered in its relation to a theory of reading instruction because the teaching of reading has come to the point now where it must be soundly based on an instructional theory." [14]

Sound-letter relationships have received immense but varying emphasis throughout the history of teaching reading. Controversy and debate about how much, when, and how to teach phoneme-grapheme relationships still continues. Even currently, the focus of such discussion is often misplaced because of a lack of accurate linguistic

---

[14]Kenneth S. Goodman, "Orthography in a Theory of Reading Instruction," *Elementary English* 49 (December, 1972):1254.

understanding of how phonology and orthography function in reading. We are most concerned when assumptions regarding the power of knowledge of sound-letter correspondences result in inappropriate instruction. Processing print to extract meaning involves use of more of the language information contained in the written language than that which is contained in sound-letter relationships alone. As early as 1908 in one of the most comprehensive explorations of the psychology of the teaching of reading, Huey presented statements that made it clear that the reading process could not be explained on the basis of simple sound-letter or word-to-word associations. He hypothesized, instead, that reading required a kind of cognitive projection that would interact with the reader's selection of certain graphic elements.[15]

In a recent exploration of the process of reading, Frank Smith stressed selectivity of the reader in processing information, and he minimized the role of the sound-letter relationship in the process of selection. This selection process, he said, depends on cognitive expectancies and a selection of recognizable units of language on the basis of distinctive features.[16] In his detailed analysis of the reading process in *Understanding Reading,* Smith commented that it is impossible to learn the sound of a word by building up from the sounds of letters. A reader's expectations about meaning, as well as past experience and ability to draw upon established language recognition categories operate simultaneously in the reading process.

When reading is conceptualized as the processing of written language for the purpose of communication, graphophonic information is *one* source of information a reader uses in extracting meaning from print. Overemphasis on sound-letter relationships may prohibit some children from acquiring appropriate strategies for making use of all available language information. This may happen because teaching sound-letter relationships has often occurred in contexts where little or no meaning is present, where inappropriate content has been taught, or where there has been little or no opportunity for children to apply the sound-letter relationships they have learned to reading situations. Divorcing study of sound-letter relationships and patterns of sound-letter relationships from meaningful communication results in the teaching of skills in isolation which, unfortunately, often has little transfer to meaningful reading. Teachers should not be deluded about the importance of "phonics;" the extent to which readers use what is taught in "phonics" may be much less than many teachers would acknowledge.

Appropriate emphasis on sound-letter relationships would help children use that knowledge in conjunction with strategies for making use of syntactic and semantic information. In planning instruction in reading and writing consistent with integrating graphophonic information and syntactic and semantic information, we suggest teachers adhere to the following guidelines:

The teaching of graphophonic information should always be related to meaning. Teaching phonics should integrate contextual situations in helping children to apply phoneme-grapheme relationships in unlocking unknown words *in a reading situation.* As Stauffer stated in a chapter on word attack skills, "Meaning directs the whole

---

[15]Edmund B. Huey, *The Psychology and Pedagogy of Reading* (Cambridge, Mass.: The MIT Press, 1968, First printing, Macmillan Co., 1908).

[16]Frank Smith, *Understanding Reading: A Psycholinguistic Analysis of Reading and Learning to Read* (New York: Holt, Rinehart and Winston, Inc., 1971), p. 74.

process." [17] Unfortunately, much teaching of phonics works with drill on letter and word units apart from a reading situation with the result that some children never apply what they have been taught because they were never taught in a reading context. Many existing materials such as phonics kits and phonics workbooks are inappropriate and indefensible materials to be used in teaching reading. Marking pictures and underlining words are not useful in helping children develop strategies for obtaining meaning while they are learning to decode print. A more useful procedure in phonics lessons would be work with contextual material with sentences containing one unfamiliar word which exemplifies the sound-letter relationship being taught. For example, when children are learning the sound-letter association for the consonant *b,* the teacher could present context sentences with all known words except for one beginning with *b.* Examples might be "I can ride my *bike* to school" or "Can you hit the *ball* with a *bat?*"

Also useful are cloze-type exercises. These can show the use of the first letter (with the rest of the word deleted) to show graphophonic information in connection with meaningful reading material. *The b_____ rang. It was time for school. The b_____ and girls came into the room. B_____ was late.*

The teaching of graphophonic information should emphasize the graphic representations of spelling patterns in meaningful words.   The isolation of separate sounds and letters distorts language and is an indefensible procedure even in teaching phoneme-grapheme relationships. Working with units of single sounds and letters cannot be supported for two major reasons. Children cannot recognize patterns when they work with units smaller than syllables. The regularity of English spelling is much greater when the unit used is a morphemic one where patterns can be discovered. Another major reason is that the language processing done by readers is not a letter-by-letter analysis. Skilled readers do not break down words into sound components and then blend them into pronounceable units. Smith claimed that fluent reading—the normal reading of a proficient reader—does not involve decoding from writing to sound. The features of written language are related directly to meaning, not to sound. [18] Teaching beginners to work with separate letters or to say that they go through phonic analysis seems unfounded. Gudschinsky reported that such a procedure was resorted to by only the poorest readers and that this procedure was not helpful. In her study of reading in many languages, she reported that sounding out each letter in isolation resulted in as many syllables as a word had letters. [19]

Although we object to separate letter and sound emphasis, we do not object to instruction in phoneme-grapheme correspondences but advocate that *instruction promote discovery of patterns of the language.* For teaching examples, teachers should select monosyllabic words containing common phonograms to illustrate the

---

[17] Russell G. Stauffer, *The Language Experience Approach to Reading Instruction* (New York: Harper and Row, 1970), p. 180.

[18] Frank Smith, "Phonology and Orthography: Reading and Writing," *Elementary English* 49 (November, 1972):1084.

[19] Sarah C. Gudschinsky, "Psycholinguistics and Reading: Diagnostic Observation," in William K. Durr, ed., *Reading Difficulties: Diagnosis, Correction and Remediation,* (Newark, Del.: International Reading Association, 1970), p. 156.

specific correspondence to be mastered since one syllable words are more regular than polysyllabic words in spelling patterns.

It is grossly inefficient to teach each word as a separate entity in reading and spelling. Thus, the skill of letter substitution can help children learn patterns to enlarge both their reading and spelling vocabularies. For example, children should realize the similarities and differences in words such as *goat, coat, float;* or *bat, bad, bag;* or *like, Luke, lake.*

The base of spelling instruction should be expanded from a narrow phoneme-grapheme base to a more comprehensive linguistic base. Hanna, Hodges, and Hanna described a linguistically based spelling program as one which includes a "phonological, morphological, and contextual (syntax-meaning) analysis." [20] Weir and Venezky claimed that ". . . the major emphasis in teaching the relationship between spelling and sound should center on the spelling-to-morpheme patterns." [21] They stressed that this principle should function in the selection of words for spelling instruction, not as rules to be learned. Carol Chomsky also reported that it is lexical features, not the single graphemic units, which relate to meaning. [22] Words such as *precede* and *precedent* or *major* and *majority* illustrate the morphophonemic base of spelling. A change in the base word form results in a pronunciation shift for a particular letter, but the morphemic considerations clue the reader and the speller. Merely explaining letter-sound correspondences of certain vowel representations is not useful here.

Teachers should understand the concepts that combinations and positions of letters provide relevant clues for recognition and for spelling. For example, *gh* in *laugh* may represent the sound normally associated with *f,* but the *gh* grapheme never represents *f* at the beginnings of words. Another example of the importance of word patterns is indicated in words such as *cap* and *cape,* both of which fit regular spelling patterns.

Instruction in spelling must help children develop the visual imagery necessary to be successful spellers. Helping children internalize a system of distinctive features for word discrimination in reading and for reproduction in spelling requires more than instruction in sound-letter correspondences and more than instruction in spelling patterns. Visual imagery should be combined with linguistic structure of spelling patterns for effective instruction.

The graphophonic content included in reading and spelling should have an accurate linguistic base. The teaching of generalizations which are erroneous or frequently not applicable should be omitted from the elementary curriculum. The content to be included in the graphophonic category of language has come under considerable scrutiny in recent years. Stemming from Clymer's[23] investigation, which reported that

---

[20]Paul R. Hanna, Richard E. Hodges, and Jean S. Hanna, *Spelling: Structure and Strategies* (Boston: Houghton-Mifflin Company, 1971), p. 121.

[21]Ruth H. Weir and Richard L. Venezky, "English Orthography: More Reason than Rhyme," in Kenneth S. Goodman, ed., *The Psycholinguistic Nature of the Reading Process,* (Detroit: Wayne State University Press, 1969), p. 199.

[22]Carol Chomsky, "Reading, Writing, and Phonology," *Harvard Educational Review* 40 (May, 1970): 287-309.

[23]Theodore Clymer, "The Utility of Phonic Generalizations in the Primary Grades," *The Reading Teacher* 16 (January, 1963):252-58.

certain generalizations were inappropriate and of low utility, evidence has mounted that phonic content offered in reading and spelling needs reevaluation. As additional linguistic information is available and as study continues on the process of reading, there should be a better informational base to determine which phonological and orthographical content is valuable.

The publication, *Spelling: Structure and Strategies* by Hanna, Hodges, and Hanna[24] offers linguistically accurate information to follow in teaching both spelling and phonics. The book cited outlines instructional programs with definite statements of content and sequence. Although the linguistic accuracy of some of the statements studied by Clymer can now be questioned, his work was a contribution in that it resulted in a questioning of what should be included in word attack instruction.

The teaching of graphophonic information should be based on helping children match spoken language to printed language.   Variations in pronunciation should be acknowledged in phonics instruction. Relationships between sound and symbol are the key. For example, if *pin* and *pen* are pronounced identically by the children, then selecting *pen* to illustrate a glided (short) sound not said by the children is an inexcusable example of not adjusting instruction according to the language background of the children. The purpose of instruction in graphophonic information is not speech correction but instead to teach sound-letter relationships. Speakers of any dialect of English need to learn how the words and sentence patterns they speak are represented in print. Regardless of how a child may pronounce a word, he needs to associate that pronunciation with its printed form. Although the printed form does not change from one reading book to another and although all readers must learn the standard orthographical system, neglecting readers' oral language background in the teaching of graphophonic information may confuse some learners.

The teaching of graphophonic information should include attention to auditory discrimination in prereading.   Teachers may comment on the lack of auditory discrimination by kindergarten and first grade children. However, if children have learned speech, they possess the auditory discrimination to learn speech and to distinguish differences in phonemes and differences in both the reception and production of oral language. For example, a child will not say *log* for *dog* or *car* for *can.* Yet, teachers may erroneously assume that a child is deficient in auditory discrimination when the real difficulty may be that he may not comprehend the concepts and terminology the teacher uses—*sound, letter, beginning of words, rhyming.* The student can use language, but prior to prereading instruction he has probably not dissected language in terms of separate phonemic units. Too much instructional time is wasted by not recognizing the auditory performance children do exhibit. Perhaps the new terminology and concepts should be presented in context with experience-type reading instead of artificial prereading instruction.

Sometimes, instruction in prereading and beginning reading introduces phoneme-grapheme relationships before children have learned to *focus* on likenesses and differences in sounds in words. If a child is unclear about which of a group of words is different from others at the beginning (examples; David, Sally, Donna), it seems

[24]Paul Hanna, Richard E. Hodges, and Jean Hanna, *Spelling: Structure and Strategies* (Boston: Houghton-Mifflin Co., 1971).

appropriate to stress the focusing of auditory discrimination on likenesses and differences before proceeding to the teaching of phoneme-grapheme correspondences.

Appropriate visual discrimination training should be offered in prereading and beginning reading. The focus in prereading and beginning reading stages should be on helping children acquire appropriate strategies for analyzing written language. Some research supports that many five- and six-year-old children have good visual discrimination and that some visual discrimination task instruction may not be needed by many kindergarten and first grade children.[25]   However, since visual discrimination of letters and words is important in learning to read, it is essential that prereading programs place emphasis on visual discrimination for those children who need such instruction. This instruction should utilize letters and words instead of nonword forms since learning to discriminate letters and words is applicable to learning to read, but training in nonword forms such as pictures, objects and geometric forms is not related to the discrimination required in reading.[26] Furthermore, the training should be both simultaneous and successive. *Simultaneous discrimination* refers to matching words or letters with an example while both the stimulus and example are visible. The *successive discrimination* task is that of locating a particular letter or word on a chart or other graphic display after the stimulus is removed from view.[27]

The teaching of graphophonic information should integrate writing activities with reading instruction, starting with the prereading and beginning reading stages of instruction.   Learning to write is part of learning the graphic symbol code. Most of the focus in this book is on linguistic foundations of reading, but a study of the process of learning to read should also consider the learning of the written symbols used in both writing and reading. The integration of writing with reading should be stressed in prereading and beginning reading as well as at higher levels.

The purpose of both writing and reading is communication of meaning. If handwriting and spelling are viewed and presented as isolated tasks focusing on reproduction of letters and words, children will probably not view writing as a process through which they may convey meanings. Children should also realize that when the teacher records experience stories the writing represents meaning. In chapter 4, incorporating the teaching of writing with beginning reading was recommended. (See page 41.)

In beginning writing, it is recommended that teachers have children write a meaningful idea instead of practicing on isolated letter forms. For example, when giving direct instruction in manuscript writing, an oral discussion about a topic can ensue from which a short three or four word sentence can be selected. The reason for controlling the length is that the situation in initial writing instruction should be of relatively short duration. The control of length in no way reflects an attempt to present a "controlled vocabulary." A sentence such as *Our fish can swim* might be chosen, and the teacher would demonstrate and explain the letter formation and spacing. Each

---

[25]Edward Paradis and Joseph Peterson, "Readiness Training Implications from Research." *The Reading Teacher* 28 (February, 1975):445–48.

[26]Thomas C. Barrett, "The Relationship between Measures of Pre-reading Visual Discrimination and First Grade Reading Achievement, A Review of the Literature," *Reading Research Quarterly* 1 (Fall, 1965): 57–76.

[27]S. Jay Samuels, "Success and Failure in Learning to Read: A Critique of the Research," *Reading Research Quarterly* 8 (Winter, 1973):216–17.

child can be directed to write each letter after the teacher demonstrates. After the writing is complete, it is important to read the sentence and to convey the concept that the writing represents an idea.

The encoding of meaning is an important consideration as children acquire the fundamentals of reproducing the symbols used in the writing system. An effective program of spelling instruction can only occur where there are functional and creative activities in which children feel a need to communicate through written expression, thus having a use for the mechanics of handwriting and spelling.

Concluding Statement

In the past, linguistic applications to reading have been most evident in the teaching of phoneme-grapheme relationships. The teaching of these relationships should include spelling patterns and morphemic units as well as sound-letter relationships. Attention to the major spelling patterns of the language in both reading and spelling is *part* of the instruction in reading which can help children to acquire effective systems for attacking unfamiliar words. The teaching of phonology and orthography should not seek to present skills in isolation but to help children to deal with contextual reading situations.

Linguistic study provides an accurate informational base about the phonology and orthography of language. Linguistic study may also reveal that certain content commonly taught will need to be revised or discarded. Our concern with reading instruction is that accurate linguistic information will be coupled with knowledge about how a reader uses graphophonic cues in the search for meaning in the reading process.

Suggested Readings

Chomsky, Carol. "Reading, Writing, and Phonology," *Harvard Educational Review* 40 (May 1970):287–309. Chomsky explores the complexity of English orthography and phonology and ties this complexity to learning written language.

Durkin, Dolores. *Strategies for Identifying Words.* Boston: Allyn and Bacon, 1976. This source explains phonics and other word analysis strategies thought to be important for teachers of reading. For the reader who wishes to study the content expected to be known by elementary teachers, this self-instructional guide will be useful.

Gibson, Eleanor and Levin, Harry. *The Psychology of Reading.* Cambridge, Mass.: MIT Press, 1975. Gibson and Levin discuss phonology and orthography in chapter 4, "Linguistic Concepts Necessary to Study Reading", but also consider these topics in relation to language development, to the reading process, and to the teaching of reading in other chapters.

Hanna, Paul R., Hodges, Richard E. and Hanna, Jean S. *Spelling: Structure and Strategies.* Boston: Houghton Mifflin Company, 1971. This book on spelling contains much information about the nature of English phonology and orthography. The book also describes recommended spelling instruction for the elementary grades.

Venezky, Richard L. "English Orthography: Its Graphical Structure and Its Relation to Sound." *Reading Research Quarterly* 2 (Spring 1967): 75–105. For those seeking detailed information about the relationships between the orthography and phonology of English. This source is recommended. The complexity of the relationships is well stated in this detailed article.

Wardhaugh, Ronald. "Linguistics and Phonics," in *Resources in Reading-Language Instruction.* Ruddell, Robert B., et al. eds., Englewood Cliffs, N.J.: Prentice-Hall, Inc., 1974, pp. 275–80. Wardhaugh states that "phonetic misinformation abounds" and calls for an accurate linguistic base in the research on and in the teaching of phonics.

The Linguistic Base for Comprehension

Comprehending ideas, feelings, attitudes, beliefs or information encoded in written language is the reader's task. Comprehending is a highly complex task and, although much has been written about comprehending, much remains to be learned. To examine the nature of reading comprehension requires that the linguistic base for communication of meaning be examined.

The linguistic base for comprehension has both semantic and syntactic foundations that interact with each other and with information from the graphophonic category. Only recently has the work of linguists in the exploration of syntactic structure and of lexical meaning been applied to the study of reading comprehension.

In this chapter we will explore the linguistic base for reading comprehension and provide a view of reading comprehension as a goal, a product, and a process. Following a discussion of both the syntactic and semantic bases of comprehension, we will suggest guidelines for instruction which are consistent with our conceptualization of reading as a language-processing activity.

The Importance of a Linguistic Base for Comprehension

Linguistic contributions to the teaching of reading must include explanations of how meaning is represented and transmitted through the language medium. Much has been written about language as a tool for communication, and much has also been written about the importance of meaning in reading. Yet, it can be noted that until recently linguistic influence in the area of comprehension in reading has received much less attention than have phonological and orthographical concerns.

Psycholinguistic definitions of reading include consideration of comprehension. Wardhaugh described reading as "the processing of information",[1] and Goodman used the phrase "reconstruction of a message from print."[2] Frank Smith used "reduction of uncertainty" as his key phrase for reading comprehension saying that the process of meaning identification is greatly dependent on the information about both the content and language form a reader already possesses and which he relies on in the reading situation.[3] Reading involves the transmission of a message from an author to a reader. The transmission process implies meaning. The author encoded a meaningful message; the reader must reconstruct a meaningful message. The medium for communication is the language code that a reader must process for meaning. The language symbols do not have meaning; they are symbols for transmitting meaning. Otto, McMenemy, and Smith stated that ". . . reading is not a symbol system, but rather the operation of that system to get meaning."[4] In comprehending, a reader must process the written language to reconstruct an author's message, and in so doing, must draw upon his knowledge of conceptual, semantic, and syntactic background.

Research in comprehension has been limited in amount until recently. In a research review in 1969 Clymer noted that research in comprehension was meager in comparison to research on word recognition.[5] In a summary of research needs, Chall stressed the need for research on the reading comprehension process and on the best strategies for teaching reading comprehension.[6] In Simon's analysis of the research on comprehension, the lack of research information on the process is evident. He commented that linguistic theory holds promise for opening a new perspective on reading comprehension. In calling for a linguistic theory of comprehension Simons stated that

> the workings of the mind while comprehending written material are a great mystery despite the voluminous research on the subject in the past half century. As a result, when children today are taught to understand what they read, the instructional procedures and materials used are based more on the intuitions and accumulated experience of reading teachers than on research evidence.[7]

He commented further that

> all the research has not shed much light on reading comprehension, mainly because the comprehension skills upon which the research has been based have tended to be

[1]Ronald Wardhaugh, *Reading: A Linguistic Perspective* (New York: Harcourt, Brace, and World Inc., 1969), p. 52.

[2]Kenneth S. Goodman, *The Psycholinguistic Nature of the Reading Process* (Detroit: Wayne State University Press, 1968), p. 15.

[3]Frank Smith, *Understanding Reading: A Psycholinguistic Analysis of Reading and Learning to Read* (New York: Holt, Rinehart, and Winston, 1971), pp. 185–210.

[4]Wayne Otto, Richard McMenemy, and Richard J. Smith, *Corrective and Remedial Reading* (Boston: Houghton-Mifflin Company, 1973), p. 140.

[5]Theodore Clymer, "How Good is Research in Reading?" in Nila B. Smith, ed., *Current Issues in Reading,* (Newark, Delaware: International Reading Association, 1969), p. 4.

[6]Jeanne B. Chall, "School Age Programs: Modifications of Teaching Methods and Materials for Total Population Groups," in Eloise O. Calkins, ed., *Reading Forum,* (Bethesda, Md.: National Institute of Neurological Diseases and Stroke, 1971), p. 196.

[7]Herbert D. Simons, "Reading Comprehension: The Need for a New Perspective," *Reading Research Quarterly* 6 (Spring, 1971): 338–63.

global and vague. Consequently, a good description of the comprehension process has not been provided.[8]

Simons argued that the major reason for the inability of researchers to focus on specific aspects of comprehension has been the lack of a theory of language.

Durkin made an important point in regard to the importance of language in comprehension when she stated that ". . . many reading comprehension problems are symptoms of deficiencies in the ability to comprehend spoken language."[9] Language-based reading instruction gives attention to comprehension in both spoken and written language. When a student has difficulty with reading comprehension, one area to be investigated is his comprehension of oral language.

Past discussions of reading comprehension have given insufficient attention to the language—the communication system. Reading has been described as a communication process, but in comprehension discussions attention has been placed on the result of reading—the message obtained—with little attention to how the language signals meaning or how the reader must process the symbol system to reconstruct a message.

How does a reader obtain meaning from print? How can teachers help children get meaning from reading? What language processing strategies are useful? How is meaning represented in language? What language information and what linguistic performance and competence are operating in the reconstruction process? How can a linguistic view of reading add to our understanding of the comprehension act and to our attempts to teach children to reconstruct meaningful messages from print? The answers to the preceding questions are not yet complete, but linguistic study must be consulted as a source for partial answers.

The contributions of linguists in understanding comprehension in reading are emerging and expanding as more information about language and language processing is becoming available. Yet, there is existing information that is not generally applied to reading instructional situations. Linguistic information related to semantics and syntax is of particular relevance in understanding the information processing task of reading.

Reading Comprehension—the Goal, the Product, the Process

Reading comprehension is the understanding of ideas represented in print. The immense importance of the comprehension dimension of reading is acknowledged in most discussions of teaching reading found in professional textbooks, in manuals accompanying teaching materials, in papers presented at national and local conferences, and in standardized and informal measures of reading performance. Until recently, however, little distinction was made between *what* was comprehended and *how* it was comprehended. Here, comprehension will be discussed as a goal of reading, as a process of comprehending, and as a product which reflects understanding in reading.

---

[8]Herbert D. Simons, "Linguistic Skills and Reading Comprehension," in Howard A. Klein, ed., *The Quest for Competency in Teaching Reading,* (Newark, Delaware: International Reading Association, 1972), p. 165.

[9]Dolores Durkin, *Teaching Them to Read* (Boston: Allyn and Bacon, Inc., 1974), p. 394.

The purpose of reading is to comprehend—to gain information, insight, and understanding. A goal of school reading programs is to help readers develop depth in comprehending printed material. In the instruction given to children in school settings, the focus should be on understanding; reading instruction should be meaning centered. Although the significance of comprehension cannot be overstated, we feel the goal may not be as fully realized as many teachers would hope because there has been a lack of attention to the process and in some cases to the lack of distinction between product and process.

The terms *comprehension* and *comprehending* can be used to distinguish between the product and the process—*comprehension* denotes product, and *comprehending* indicates the act or process itself. Simons used this distinction when he claimed that a linguistic perspective should be one that focuses on the process instead of measuring the product.

> The comprehension process is the mental operations which take place in the reader's head while he is reading. These operations are generally not observable and not open to introspection. On the other hand, the products of the comprehension process are the behaviors produced after comprehension has taken place, such as answers to test questions.[10]

Although the process is elusive, reading theoreticians and practitioners need to strive to understand more about that process and be aware of the distinction between the product and process. In the teaching of reading comprehension, attention has been given to the product while relatively little has been substantiated about the process. For example, in a directed reading situation children are usually questioned about what they read, and their responses are used by the teacher to indicate their understanding. Although such a procedure is recommended and does encourage children to interpret, react to, and recall what has been read, this is an example of focus on the *product.* The process also deserves study. In examining children's responses to what is read, teachers have been concerned with the evidence of the product of comprehension but may be unaware of what happens in the reconstruction of meaning from a printed passage. If the product dimension reflects weaknesses, some reasons for poor performance may be found in examination of the *processing* done by individuals.

A definition of the process of comprehension which stresses the linguistic base was given by Carroll.

> Comprehension, whether of speech or writing, is a process not completely understood and difficult to describe briefly, in any case. It can be described linguistically as a process of comprehending morphemes (minimal meaning units) and the grammatical constructions in which they occur. The lexical meanings of morphemes can be stated in terms of objective referents and their attributes and relationships.[11]

In comprehending, there is always an interaction between the reader and the material being processed. Wardhaugh noted that

---

[10]Herbert D. Simons, "Reading Comprehension: The Need for a New Perspective," *Reading Research Quarterly* 6 (Spring, 1971):340.

[11]John B. Carroll, "A Psycholinguistic Analysis of Reading Behavior" in Albert J. Harris and Edward R. Sipay, eds., *Readings on Reading Instruction* (New York: David McKay Co., Inc., 1972), p. 53.

comprehension is not a passive process. The comprehender must continually make hypotheses about what he is hearing or reading, attempt to match these hypotheses with other data he has available to him, and modify the hypotheses if they are inadequate.[12]

One of the most cited descriptions of comprehension is that of Thorndike. He described comprehension as

> . . . a very elaborate procedure, involving a weighing of each of many elements in a sentence, their organization in the proper relations to one another, the selection of certain of their connotations and the rejection of others, and the cooperation of many forces to determine final response.[13]

The process of comprehending is one in which a reader searches for meaning, selects cues from the printed message, and makes predictions about the content. Many factors other than linguistic ones operate in both comprehending and comprehension, and we do not mean to imply that comprehension is exclusively a linguistic process. Information about cognitive processing and the interrelationships of thought and language are of immense importance in understanding in reading. Comprehending and comprehension are both related to what a reader brings to the reading situation. According to Carroll, "Problems of reading comprehension appear to arise mainly when texts contain lexical, grammatical, or ideational materials which happen to be outside the reader's repertory."[14]

Smith acknowledged that the greater the familiarity of a reader with the content of the material being read, the less the dependency of the reader on the visual information.[15] Linguistically based reading instruction also acknowledges the effect of prior experience and conceptual development on the reconstruction of meaning. However, in addition to experiential and conceptual background and individual interests, abilities, and attitudes, a reader also brings to the task the sum total of his linguistic performance and competence.

Focusing on the process of comprehension is more difficult than discussing the goal and product of comprehension. Yet, it is this intriguing process that must be better understood to improve the teaching of reading. Wardhaugh noted that grammarians have long been concerned with how sentences make sense—but unable to describe the "sense-making process."

> Comprehension requires far more than understanding the meaning of individual words and then fusing these meanings by some mysterious process so that sense will result. It is this process, this fusion itself, that requires a close examination, about which the linguist provides important information.[16]

---

[12]Ronald Wardhaugh, *Reading: A Linguistic Perspective* (New York: Harcourt, Brace and World, Inc., 1969), p. 137.

[13]Edward L. Thorndike, "Reading as Reasoning: A Study of Mistakes in Paragraph Reading," *Reading Research Quarterly* 6 (Summer, 1971):425.

[14]John B. Carroll, "A Psycholinguistic Analysis of Reading Behavior" in Albert J. Harris and Edward R. Sipay, eds., *Readings on Reading Instruction,* (New York: David McKay Co., Inc., 1972), p. 53.

[15]Frank Smith, *Understanding Reading: A Psycholinguistic Analysis of Reading and Learning to Read* (New York: Holt, Rinehart and Winston, Inc., 1971), pp. 185–210.

[16]Ronald Wardhaugh, *Reading: A Linguistic Perspective* (New York: Harcourt, Brace and World, Inc., 1969), pp. 63, 66.

The Syntactic Base for Comprehension

Syntax refers to the arrangement of morphemes into grammatical phrases and sentences in a language. Moulton described the function of syntax as that of arranging morphemes in such a way as to produce meaningful sentences.[17] The grammar or syntax of a language is the essential link in communication between meaning and sound or meaning and symbol. Deese also described the syntax of a language as the bridge between the sound system and the semantic or meaning system in the language.[18] Langacher defined syntax as the set of principles that makes it possible to combine lexical items in grammatically acceptable and comprehensible sentences.[19]

The patterning or arrangement of words in meaningful sentence units is language information crucial to understanding spoken and written language. Yet, the application of this information in the teaching of reading is meager. Lefevre claimed that

> so far there has been no systematic effort to base reading theory and methodology on anything approaching what we know about sentence patterns, intonation, and other important elements of the structural system of English.[20]

Rystrom noted that

> many American linguists have been interested in the syntax of English, and many reading specialists have felt that the structure of the language plays a pivotal role in the reading process; yet almost no research has examined the specific ways in which the structure of language influences the process through which children learn to read.[21]

The work of Menyuk substantiates that children do acquire the syntactic patterns of the language in the preschool years.[22] Thus, it is possible to state that children have linguistic performance and competence in both comprehending and producing the syntactic patterns of the native language before learning to read. (See page 24.) However, it is well to keep in mind that syntactic complexity can interfere with comprehension. Carol Chomsky's work with the acquisition of syntax in children from five to ten revealed that children in this age group have difficulty with the interpretation of syntactic structures of a relatively complex nature. She made an important point when she noted that

> the nature of children's observed mistakes in interpreting a number of structures is important in bringing out various aspects of the implicit linguistic knowledge which they

[17]William G. Moulton, "The Study of Languge and Human Communication," in Albert H. Marckwardt, ed, *Linguistics in School Programs,* 69th Yrbk., Part II, National Society for the Study of Education Education (Chicago: The University of Chicago Press, 1970), p. 18.

[18]James Deese, *Psycholinguistics* (Boston: Allyn and Bacon, Inc., 1970), p. 1.

[19]Ronald W. Langacker, *Language and its Structure* (New York: Harcourt, Brace, Jovanovich, Inc., 1973), pp. 29–30, 90.

[20]Carl A. Lefevre, "A Multidisciplinary Approach to Language and Reading" in Kenneth S. Goodman, ed., *The Psycholinguistic Nature of the Reading Process* (Detroit: Wayne State University Press, 1968), pp. 298–99.

[21]Richard Rystrom, "Linguistics and the Teaching of Reading," *Journal of Reading Behavior* 4 (Winter, 1972):36.

[22]Paula Menyuk, *Sentences Children Use* (Cambridge, Mass.: The MIT Press, 1969).

do possess. For we find that the children do in fact assign an interpretation to the structures that we present to them. They do not, as they see it, fail to understand our sentences. They understand them, but they understand them wrongly.[23]

The speculation in this chapter is that problems in interpretation of reading material can in part be due to wrong interpretation of syntactic patterns. When the language of children is quite different from the syntactic patterns of reading materials, the chance of interference in the language processing task is greater than when there is a close match between the language of the reader and the material. Not only the mismatch of oral and spoken language but the complexity of syntactic patterns can be an obstacle to comprehension. Fagan expressed the underlying idea of this section, "For children to comprehend what they read, they must be able to understand the written language structures by which ideas, information and concepts are conveyed."[24]

In this discussion of the syntactic base of reading comprehension, we are discussing the unit of language useful to a reader, the concepts of deep and surface structure, and intonation features of language. Although the semantic base is not discussed until the next major section of the chapter, it should be noted that semantic considerations interact with the syntactic information and that readers use the two information systems simultaneously.

UNIT OF LANGUAGE FOR COMPREHENSION

Central to exploration of the comprehension process is examination of the units of meaning in language. The smallest identifiable meaning unit of language is the morpheme, but the minimal meaning-bearing pattern for communication is the sentence. In viewing comprehension as language processing, teachers should acknowledge that the meaning carrying patterns of language are not letters or single words but sentence units. As early as 1908 Huey stated that, "Language begins with the sentence, and this is the unit of language everywhere."[25]

Lefevre made a strong case for the sentence as the minimal meaning-bearing unit of language, and he also asserted that the basic fault in poor reading is poor sentence sense. To develop sentence sense, a reader must ". . . be made aware of the nature and structure of sentences to begin with, including sentence intonation."[26] He commented that a simplistic word-perception theory of reading is a very naïve view of the reading process.

In observing some instructional practices in teaching reading, one might conclude that the important units for language study are letters and words—not sentences. Fragmentation of language in reading instruction can make the task of meaning reconstruction difficult and may lead the beginner to regard reading as a word-identification task. The approaches to reading instruction which focus on letter and word

---

[23]Carol Chomsky, *The Acquisition of Syntax in Children from Five to Ten* (Cambridge, Mass.: The MIT Press, 1969), p. 2.

[24]William T. Fagan, "Transformations and Comprehension," *The Reading Teacher* 25 (Nov., 1971):169.

[25]Edmund B. Huey, *The Psychology and Pedagogy of Reading* (Cambridge, Mass.: The MIT Press, 1968; first printing, The Macmillan Co., 1908), p. 123.

[26]Carl A. Lefevre, "The Simplistic Standard Word-Perception Theory of Reading," *Elementary English* 45 (March, 1968):351, 349.

units may be based on the rationale that limiting and simplifying the language unit will make the task of beginning reading easier. However, such a rationale may be ill-founded since, without focus on sentence units for comprehension, readers are deprived of some of the cue systems of the language. As Goodman said, "The important point is that language—not words or morphemes—in its ordered flow is the medium of communication."[27] He also argued that the meaning of a sentence depends on the words and morphemes it contains but that sentence meaning involves more than the sum of the meanings of the lexical items. The systematic structuring of language symbols syntactically provides clues to meaning not contained solely in letters and words.

Gudschinsky also commented on the importance of meaningful language units in reading: "It is essential that good reading instruction include much practice in the reading of units larger than a single word. Word by word reading is not meaningful as evidenced by the listing intonation pattern that is used. It seems evident that the word is not the basic unit of meaning in connected material."[28]

In commenting on sentence comprehension, Lefevre called the sentence the basic building block of meaning, and he stated that comprehension begins with sentence comprehension, although he also acknowledged the importance of larger units. "Sentences in sequence within larger graphic structures (such as the paragraph) build up interrelationships into more complex meaning-bearing structures."[29] Comprehension instruction should help children develop "sentence sense" and apply their existing knowledge about the intonation of language in speech as a clue to reading.

In reading miscue research, which has examined children's performance in oral reading, Goodman reported that children do use syntactic clues as evidenced by some responses that differ from the actual print but preserve syntactic patterns.[30] For example, if you were asked to read the following sentence: *The boys were playing in the* _____. You might supply any of the following words, *house, garage, building, street, basement, field.* The syntactic arrangement and context help you in the reading task. Yet, conscious teaching of language structure clues is minimal in much reading instruction.

In examining the unit of language to be processed in reading, it is well to remember that for comprehension of ideas expressed in language readers need information from all the cue systems of language. Readers must work with meaning-bearing patterns of language, not isolated words or letters. Frank Smith wrote, "Reading does not easily lend itself to compartmentalization"[31] and Goodman stated, "Nothing less than decoding of large language units is reading."[32]

[27]Kenneth S. Goodman, "Words and Morphemes in Reading" in Kenneth S. Goodman and James T. Fleming, eds., *Psycholinguistics and the Teaching of Reading* (Newark, Delaware: International Reading Association, 1969), p. 28.

[28]Sarah C. Gudschinsky, "Psycholinguistics and Reading: Diagnostic Observations," in William K. Durr, ed., *Reading Difficulties Diagnosis, Correction and Remediation* (Newark, Delaware: International Reading Association, 1970), p. 157.

[29]Carl A. Lefevre, *Linguistics and the Teaching of Reading* (New York: McGraw-Hill Book Company, 1964), p. 81.

[30]Kenneth S. Goodman, "Analysis of Oral Reading Miscues: Applied Psycholinguistics," *Reading Research Quarterly* 5 (Fall, 1969):9–30.

[31]Frank Smith, *Psycholinguistics and Reading* (New York: Holt, Rinehart and Winston, 1973), p. 8.

[32]Kenneth S. Goodman, ed., *The Psycholinguistic Nature of the Reading Process* (Detroit: Wayne State University Press, 1968), p. 18.

Historically, the explorations of linguists into the comprehension process have concentrated on the sentence unit and less on larger units of discourse such as paragraphs and stories. Much more is needed in learning how readers interrelate, recall, classify, analyze, evaluate, and synthesize ideas from reading. These tasks are often considered to be products of comprehension instead of elements in the comprehension process, and certainly cognitive and linguistic processing must operate with language units larger than sentences.

Surface and Deep Structure

Recent developments in linguistics have led to an examination of language from a generative-transformational point of view. Language in this view is an overtly manifested representation of meaning. The manifested structure is termed *surface structure,* and the underlying meaning is termed *deep structure.* Every sentence has both a surface and deep structure. The surface structure is the form of language to which a listener or reader is exposed. It is the actual, physical form or realization—auditory signals in listening and graphic symbols in reading—that is processed in listening and reading. In order for comprehension to occur, a listener or reader must process the auditory or graphic surface structure and relate to it the appropriate deep structure.

In generative-transformational grammar, deep structure (underlying meaning) is transformed to surface structure (physical form) through the use of rules of syntax internalized by native language users. Thus, the surface structure of a sentence is composed of syntactically structured arrangements of lexical items (morphemes). The task of reading or listening is to infer the writer's or speaker's meaning by processing the syntactically ordered lexical items of the surface structure. Competence in processing the surface structures of sentences is not based only on knowledge of sound-letter relationships for while this relates phonology and orthography, syntax and conceptual background play major roles in relating surface and deep structures.

As an illustration of generative-transformational grammar, consider the idea that an Irish setter has treed a Siamese cat. This idea is the deep structure which, through application of particular transformational rules, will become surface structure. Options are available for we could say: *The dog has treed the cat; The Irish setter has treed the cat; The Siamese cat has been treed by the dog.* Listeners hear the surface structure chosen by the speaker (readers see the surface structure chosen by the writer) and process it to infer deep structure. This processing must include more than assigning meaning to individual words since assigning meaning to individual words could lead to an inappropriate deep structure such as the idea that the dog was treed by the cat. Thus, appropriate inferences regarding the deep structure are cued not only by the individual words, but also by the arrangement of these items in the surface structure. Arrangements of lexical items are governed by syntax.

The following nonsense sentence example that was developed by Kenneth Goodman can be used to illustrate the role of the deep and surface levels in language processing along with the semantic content:"The marlup was poving his kump." [33] It is

---

[33] *Ibid.,* pp. 23–24.

possible for a reader of English to easily "read" that sentence with accurate intonation because of the structure of the sentence and because of the clues provided with
the function words *the, was,* along with the ending *ing.* A reader may be able to trans-
form the surface structure so as to realize that it was the kump that was being poved,
through use of syntactic information. However, the reader is blocked in the comprehension task because of lack of semantic information since there are no conceptual
referents in his background for *marlup* or *poving* or *kump.* If the word order were
something like *Kump the poving was marlup his* there could not be syntactic processing because this is not a familiar syntactic pattern in our language. The point is that
to comprehend a reader must use both semantic and syntactic clues in interrelated
ways.

INTONATION

One feature of our language structure which is related to the syntactical system is that
of intonation. Intonation, although clearly evident in speech, is incompletely represented in the writing system. Intonation has been generally ignored as a language cue
that readers draw upon in the reading process. However, reconstruction of messages
from print as a reader recovers the meaning or deep structure does include dependence upon the intonation clues assigned to the surface structure. We are not saying
that a reader changes the print to speech, but that in language processing intonation
is one feature of syntax.

Intonation was described by Lefevre as the melodies of speech and includes the
features of pitch, stress, and juncture in spoken language.[34] The intensity of speech is
reflected by the pitch, and stress refers to the degree of emphasis or accent with which
syllables, words, and parts of sentences are spoken. Juncture denotes pauses in
speaking or reading. It is the feature of juncture rather than the phonemes associated
with certain letters that accounts for the difference between the way "blue bird" and
"bluebird" are spoken or in the difference between "a name" and "an aim." Junc-
tures are also indicated by punctuation signals.

Lefevre claimed that intonation is perhaps the least understood signaling system in
sentence-level utterances in English.[35] He also asserted, "Intonation as a part of
English structure, when it has not been ignored altogether, has been lost in the fog of
'reading with expression'."[36] Mountain said, "Only within the past few years have
linguists, researchers, and teachers become aware of the connections between intonation and certain kinds of reading errors."[37] She reported the following story:

> A second grade boy announced to the teacher, "I found a mistake in my book." The
> child referred to page 20 of *The King, The Mice, And The Cheese.* The picture
> showed a group of cats in hot pursuit of some mice. The text read, "The mice-chasing

---

[34]Carl A. Lefevre, *Linguistics and the Teaching of Reading* (New York: McGraw-Hill Book Company,
1964), p. 44.

[35]*Ibid.,* p. xvi.

[36]Carl A. Lefevre, "A Multidisciplinary Approach to Language and to Reading: Some Projection," in
Kenneth S. Goodman, ed., *The Psycholinguistic Nature of the Reading Process* (Detroit: Wayne State
University Press, 1968), p. 298.

[37]Lee Mountain, "Intonation for Beginners," in Carl Braun, ed., *Language, Reading, and the Communication Process* (Newark, Delaware: International Reading Association, 1970), p. 150.

cats did a very good job." The teacher asked where the mistake was. The reply, "Don't you see?" he answered impatiently. "In the picture the cats are chasing the mice. But the words say, 'The . . . mice . . . chasing . . . cats . . .' and the mice aren't chasing the cats. It's the other way around. Don't you see?"[38]

Mountain explains that the boy was reading word-for-word and had miscued by ignoring the intonation. She speculated that he wasn't at all aware of the elements of intonation in reading, although he constantly used these elements in his speech.

Much of the meaning of spoken langue is contained in the intonation system. Sustakoski wrote, "One feature frequently forgotten by designers of reading texts and by traditional grammarians is the intonational system. This system is one of the most important devices of grammar, and it signals many distinctions obvious in speech but relatively obscure on the printed page."[39] Botel wrote, "Since intonation is one of the structural systems of language, we must bring to each child's consciousness the incompleteness with which it is signalled by the writing system, so that he may expect and know how to supply or reconstruct the unrecorded melody for himself."[40] The orthography contains punctuation and capitalization clues that help the reader, but these are incomplete. Sentence-patterning or language-structure clues operate in connection with the intonation patterns.

It is well to remember that although intonation is one feature of language to be drawn upon in teaching children to use syntactic clues, adequate oral reading does not necessarily mean adequate grasp of meaning. Burke and Goodman reported that intonation in oral reading seems to be a quite stable factor in reading and that intonation may remain acceptable even when the comprehension is poor.[41] They speculate that intonation is the first aspect of speech an infant develops and, as such, should be stable.

As we have already noted, children come to school with the acquisition of the basic syntactic patterns of the language. Children naturally employ intonation as they speak and as they interpret the ideas of others. What may be difficult for some children to realize is that the written language is to be read with natural speech inflections.

The Semantic Base for Comprehension

Linguists use the term *semantics* to refer to the study of the meaning system of language, and it includes the study of how words and sentences are related to conceptual entities in the real world and the ways in which words and sentences are related to one another. According to Bolinger, the point at which language makes contact with the outside world is called *meaning*.[42] However, just how language makes this contact

---

[38] *Ibid.*, p. 149.

[39] Henry J. Sustakoski, "Some Contributions of Linguistic Science to the Teaching of Reading," in James Walden, ed., *Oral Language and Reading* (Champaign, Illinois: National Council of Teachers of English, 1969), p. 63.

[40] Morton Botel, "What Linguistics Says to the This Teacher of Reading and Spelling," *The Reading Teacher* 18 (Dec., 1964):188–89.

[41] Carolyn Burke and Kenneth S. Goodman, "When A Child Reads: A Psycholinguistic Analysis," *Elementary English* 47 (Jan., 1970):127.

[42] Dwight Bolinger, *Aspects of Language* (New York: Harcourt, Brace and World, 1968), p. 219.

with the real world is not completely understood. Langacker cautioned: "to describe meaning, or even what sort of thing this meaning is, we are forced to talk about the structure of thought and cognition." [43] He explained further, "While we can with some assurance say quite a bit about the relation between meaning and strings of morphemes, there are many large and serious gaps in our knowledge." [44] Burke, in discussing the semantic system of language, stated that meaning "has received the least attention—not because the linguists have failed to recognize its significance, but because they recognized its complexity." [45]

Unfortunately, much of the discussion of meaning in reading instruction has assumed a rather narrow view of meaning, focused on words and word meanings under rather hazy discussions of getting meaning from print. Emphasis has been on vocabulary development treating words as if they existed in isolation rather than in contextual arrangements. Although the development of an extensive reading vocabulary is certainly one aspect of reading instruction, study of words and word meanings apart from meaningful and appropriate language contexts is insufficient and may be deleterious to the development of strategies for reconstructing meaning from written language.

We would not deny the importance of the oral language background and vocabulary that a reader possesses. Nor would we disagree that the conceptual background and the richness of association of meaning with one's stock of vocabulary influences to a great degree the meaning one can extract from written language. Indeed, if words encountered in reading are unfamiliar in meaning, the process of reconstructing meaning from written language may be thwarted. However, in many instances too much attention has been paid to the teaching of individual words out of whole-language contexts.

The nonsense sentence about the marlup illustrates one aspect of the lack of availability of the meaning system. In this sentence, even though the orthography utilizes sound-letter relationships found in English and the inflectional and syntactic systems of English, there are no conceptual entities—no real-world objects or processes—for *marlup, poving, kump* to which these "words" are related. Without referents in the real world the sentence is meaningless. An utterance, sentence, or passage in a language is meaningful only if it contains "words" for which there are conceptual referents in the mind of the language user. In addition, however, the reader must know the meanings resulting from the relationships cued by the arrangement of words and the syntactic information within words.

The semantic and syntactic systems operate in an interrelated fashion providing the reader with lexical and relational meaning through the interaction. Lexical meaning is indeed necessary, but it may be insufficient for proficient reading in which appropriate interpretations are made. Carol Chomsky's work on the acquisition of syntactic competence illustrates this point rather clearly. Her research showed that although children could define the word *promise* (that is they knew its "meaning"), when promise occurred in sentences like *John promised Mary to shovel the driveway* many

[43]Ronald W. Langacker, *Language and Its Structure* (New York: Harcourt, Brace Jovanovich, Inc., 1973), p. 90.

[44]*Ibid.*, p. 90.

[45]Carolyn L. Burke, "The Language Process: System or Systematic?" in Richard A. Hodges and E. Hugh Rudorf, eds., *Language and Learning to Read: What Teachers Should Know About Language* (Boston: Houghton Mifflin Company, 1972), p. 24.

children interpreted the sentence as *John told* Mary to shovel the driveway—that Mary, not John, was to do the shoveling. From this evidence, Chomsky concluded that knowledge of a word is not complete until "on the one hand the speaker knows the concept attached to the word, and secondly he knows the constructions with which the word can enter"[46] and thus, can discern appropriate relationships among the concepts represented by the words. In this sense, the meaning of a word may be regarded as the result of the meaning of the sentence as well as contributing to the meaning of the sentence. Consequently, word meaning per se may be considered insufficient for proficient reading without the knowledge of and use of relational meanings as cues through which the intended relationships among ideas are signalled. Accordingly, if the semantic cues of word meaning and relational meaning are not well used, understanding an author's message may be severely limited.

At the risk of oversimplification, we should here like to present one conceptualization of the role of meaning in reading. From a language processing view of reading, the activity that takes place during reading is the formulation of a series of conjectures about meaning derived from knowledge of sound-letter relationships, intuitive knowledge of the English word-order restrictions and knowledge of lexical and relational meanings all of which are tested and verified (or reformulated) by the reader's endeavor to uncover meaning. The reader uses all derived meaning to formulate subsequent hypotheses about words, grammatical sequences and additional meaning, then processes the orthography and derives more meaning. The reader is, in a sense, pulled toward meaning if the series of conjectures he makes are more frequently confirmed than disconfirmed, if the purposes for reading are meaningful, and if the processing yields the sort of meaningfulness to which the reader can relate.

In our opinion, helping children learn to make use of the meaning system of language may be facilitated under two general conditions. First, the learner must learn to read with written language material that is potentially meaningful to him. Nonsense words or real words in nonsensical (to him) sentences are not, and cannot be, comprehensible in the fullest sense because these do not provide semantic (lexical and relational) clues to meaning. Second, readers must learn to make active use of the meaning they have obtained as they process written language in order to predict both grammatical sequences and meaning. Meaning cannot be considered solely as the *product* of reading; rather the processing of meaning cues must occur such that the semantic system serves as a source of information for cumulative meaning synthesized both affectively and cognitively by the reader.

Teaching Comprehension as Language Processing: Guidelines for Instruction

All teachers of reading are charged with the task of helping children understand printed messages. In the comments in this section, we will highlight guidelines based on the linguistic processing nature of comprehension, but we do not mean to imply that this is the total concern in the complex area of reading comprehension. The view of comprehension as a product will rightfully continue to be part of reading instruc-

[46]Carol Chomsky, *The Acquisition of Syntax in Children from 5 to 10,* (Cambridge, Massachussets: The MIT Press, 1969), p. 5.

tional programs. However, the process dimension of comprehension also deserves attention in the teaching of reading. The comprehending process has both cognitive and linguistic facets which are interrelated in a number of ways. Our concern here is primarily with the linguistic processing tasks, but we acknowledge the immense importance of cognitive considerations as well.

One common way of describing reading comprehension has been to identify comprehension skills. Although much of the instruction which centers around specific comprehension skills (finding the main idea, identifying specific details, following a sequence of events, inferring outcomes, etc.) is often valid, a skill focus alone may be a deterrent to children's development of integrated strategies for reading for meaning. Another major emphasis in recent years in teaching comprehension has been on levels of thinking required to obtain meaning from selections and to respond to various types of questions. As a result of taxonomic descriptions of levels of comprehension and thinking[47],[48] along with discussions of questioning strategies employed by teachers, the teaching of reading comprehension has been improved. Attention to the process should also result in improvement of instruction. Throughout the discussion of the guidelines for instruction in comprehension, the reader will note the authors' view that comprehension is the goal of all reading.

Meaning is the paramount consideration in the teaching or comprehension as language processing.   The purpose of all reading is comprehension. Instruction in reading, then, would logically be focused on this goal. Stauffer maintained, "If it is accepted that critical, creative, and versatile reading is a process akin to thinking, then instruction that will best achieve such goals is needed." [49]

Readers' purposes in reading affect comprehension. Thoughtful reading includes purpose setting and prediction prior to and during the reading act. If meaning is the paramount consideration in instruction, then focus on purposes defined and perceived by readers is essential in developing thoughtful reactions to reading. The purposes guide the process since prediction is such an important determiner of understanding. The teaching strategy of having readers speculate about selection content before reading should be employed at all levels of reading. Students, not teachers, should identify the purposes for which reading is done. Reading then becomes a reasoning act in which readers search for meaning to validate or reject their hypotheses.

When purposes direct reading, postreading discussions will center around the connection between ideas suggested in the purpose-setting discussion before reading and the ideas presented in the reading selection. The discussion is not centered on answering routine questions but is a high level critical analysis based on the learners' examination of ideas.

Comprehension should be stressed from the initial stages of reading instruction. In prereading and beginning reading, children should grasp the concept that the

---

[47]Benjamin S. Bloom, ed., *Taxonomy of Educational Objectives* (New York: David McKay Company, 1965).

[48]Richard J. Smith and Thomas Barrett, *Teaching Reading in the Middle Grades* (Reading, Mass.: Addison Wesley Publishing Company, 1974), pp. 53–57.

[49]Russell G. Stauffer, *Directing the Reading Thinking Process* (New York: Harper and Row, 1975).

purpose of written language is for communication. Comprehension does not become important only after children have learned to read; it is the primary consideration in the introduction of reading and writing. If programs for beginning reading place a higher value on the learning of graphophonic cues than on meaning, word calling often results for some learners because reading is not viewed as a process which is a search for meaning. Such word calling can be prevented if reading instruction gives priority to meaning from the very beginning of instruction. Again, we say attention to meaning and purpose does not come after children learn to read; it is the focus of learning to read.

In order to stress the communication function of reading, one recommendation is to conduct prereading and beginning reading with the language experience approach. The key to showing that written language represents meaning is to use written language materials created by recording children's spoken thoughts. Children's speech provides a link between the already familiar speech communication system and the unfamiliar written communication code. Reading is taught as language processing when a language experience approach is used with communication occuring both in the creation and reading of language experience materials. These materials help children make a match between their speech and representation of their ideas in written language. The description of reading as "talk written down" is inaccurate as a description of the reading process but does express an understanding children may internalize about the reading materials when those materials are composed by recording their oral language.

Materials for reading instruction should be comprehensible to students.   Since comprehension is so greatly influenced by a reader's prior knowledge and language processing abilities, selection of materials should be based on consideration of these factors. In order for purpose and prediction to operate optimally to promote comprehension, the material to be read should be potentially meaningful, not anomolous or meaningless, for students.

One of the reading teacher's responsibilities in developing comprehension is to help students makes a connection between prior knowledge and the ideas of any reading selection. Background discussions, raising questions, and setting purposes prior to silent reading help foster communication. Particularly when certain materials are foreign in content to the readers using them, the teacher must provide additional background for comprehension to occur.

Reading material should contain meaningful units of language. Sentences, paragraphs and longer selections are essential for the reconstruction of messages from print. In order to process information from all the cue systems of the language (graphophonic, semantic, and syntactic), a reader must deal with units no smaller than sentences. Emphasis on words or letters or sounds instead of on meaningful language is unjustifiable since such practices deprive the reader of the use of all available cues when reading sentences, paragraphs, and total selections. Isolated word and letter study is not communication, and emphasis on fragmented language leads to a gross neglect of meaning and purposeful reading.

Self-selection of reading material by students helps assure a match between material and student ability. An abundance of materials should be available in all classes in order to promote meaningful and wide reading.

The process of semantic and syntactic information should be combined.   Teaching semantic and syntactic processing together is closely related to the preceding statements stressing the use of meaningful language units. Every sentence contains semantic and syntactic clues or meaning. The semantic content of lexical items is influenced by the syntactic patterns in which they appear. Situations in which reading vocabulary is presented apart from context are inappropriate because they remove the effect of syntax on word meaning.

Helping readers process surface structure in order to recover underlying meaning should be part of teaching comprehension. Comprehension activities that require children to paraphase reading material necessitate that the deep structural level of the material be processed. Students' paraphrasing of material should reflect their understanding of the deep structure or meaning. Sentence comprehension cannot occur unless readers can recover meaning through processing the structural relationships present in surface and deep structures.

Simons explored the measurement of students' ability to recover deep structure of sentences. [50] For students who have difficulty with comprehension of sentences, the types of exercises he suggested could be useful teaching procedures. In each of his examples attention is given to the ability to recognize alternative surface structures or paraphrases for a particular sentence.

The use of intonation features of language is included in teaching comprehension as language processing.   Attention should be given to helping children learn to supply the intonation clues so natural in speech to written language. The expressionless, word-by-word reading characteristic of some children demonstrates that these children do not use intonation for communication. Such reading may result from material that is too difficult both in concepts and in the amount of unfamiliar words, but sometimes such reading results when children are taught to read with techniques which stress the word or letter unit with little attention to meaningful units of language. Words in isolation are said with distorted emphasis and do not receive the same intonation as when spoken in sentences for communication. Such distortion may be more common in beginning instruction than at higher levels, but early habits may die hard.

Writing children's speech to create reading materials in the language experience approach is one way to develop materials for teaching intonation cues. When reading materials are those children have composed, they can be taught to *consciously* apply in reading the same intonation used in speech. The conscious emphasis on intonation patterns is one difference between language experience reading and commercially prepared reading materials. Telling children to read something "like it sounds" may be an incomprehensible direction when the language of reading materials is stilted and artificial.

Readers need to know the relationship between intonation and punctuation signals. One symptom of poor reading sometimes evident in the oral reading of students who

---

[50]Herbert D. Simons, "Reading Comprehension: the Need for a New Perspective," *Reading Research Quarterly* 6 (Spring, 1971):358–60.

are poor in comprehension is disregard of punctuation. When children read sentence units with comprehension, the punctuation signals are one source of information. Stress on isolated words and letters does not lead readers to accurately use punctuation clues. Language experience materials can be useful in this respect as the use of punctuation and capitalization is shown from the initial reading stage as a part of the written representation of spoken language.

The significance of continuous language exposure and extension in improving comprehension should be recognized. Continuous language exposure and extension should be included in the total school program. This recommendation is so broad that in practice it may be ignored unless teachers have internalized and truly value the importance of a comprehensive language program and recognize the contributions of that program to effective reading and communication. The total curriculum should contribute to the fund of knowledge and to the language facility readers use to process the written language code for comprehension. The exposure and language development which adds to the ability to deal with ideas and the language encountered in reading cannot be accomplished only in the instruction directed specifically to reading.

Good language teaching provides the freedom to explore and experiment with language. In addition to the wealth of language exposure that comes through literature and wide reading, other language and curriculum activities should add to children's ability to use language. Participation in meaningful communication situations requiring thinking, listening, speaking, and writing should increase students' comprehension in reading. The good comprehender in reading should be able to use language easily for communication in both productive speaking and writing situations and in receptive listening and speaking situations. Reading comprehension is a form of language comprehension.

Readers' ability to comprehend orally should be considered in the evaluation of and in the teaching of reading comprehension. When students experience difficulty in comprehending in reading, teachers should attempt to determine if those students have the same difficulty in comprehending the same material orally or if the comprehension difficulty is only with the written form.

For students for whom the problem with comprehension occurs with both oral and written situations, the recommendations are to probe further for conceptual and language barriers, to work on oral comprehension, to enrich the background, and to adjust the choice of materials. One technique to be used for teaching sentence and story comprehension is to adapt language experience procedures so that readers can be shown the correspondence between spoken and written language. Children can be asked to interpret the experience stories of other children in an activity which works with simple comprehension of ideas with nonthreatening, easily understood materials.

For students who comprehend orally, but not in reading situations, several practices can be suggested. The purpose-setting strategy discussed earlier should be employed. The questions posed in discussions should be ones which require thoughtful responses by the reader instead of mechanical, rote answers. If children have difficulty in reading comprehension tasks yet seem to have adequate oral vocabulary, conceptual knowledge, and good word recognition skills for the material being read, paraphrasing sentences will help them process the surface structure to recover meaning. After students are accustomed to the sentence unit in comprehension, instruction can be directed to larger units.

Concluding Statement

In order to comprehend, readers must draw upon the syntactic and semantic information sources available in written language while using the sum total of their language and experiential background to do so. As one reads, meaning is the product as well as a source of information used in processing written language.

Reading instruction must build upon the learners' language and experiential background by helping them learn how to draw upon their already known language and experience in order to arrive at a meaningful interpretation of written language. Emphasis on arriving at a meaningful interpretation of written language must exist at all stages in reading instruction. Meaning must be paramount.

Suggested Readings

Carroll, John. *Language and Thought.* Englewood Cliffs, N.J.: Prentice-Hall, Inc., 1964. The interrelationships of language and thought are discussed by Carroll throughout this text. This book is recommended here since serious consideration of cognition in reading must include the function of language in the comprehending process.

Goodman, Kenneth S. "Comprehension-Centered Reading" In Ekwall, Eldon E. comp. *Psychological Factors in the Teaching of Reading.* Columbus, Ohio: Charles E. Merrill Publishing Co., 1973. As the title indicates, Goodman focuses on the significance of comprehension in reading. Teaching reading must also be focused on comprehension.

Simons, Herbert. "Reading Comprehension: The Need for a New Perspective," *Reading Research Quarterly* 6 (Spring 1971):338–63. Simons presents a case for the need for a linguistic base for understanding comprehension. He reviews previous perspectives on reading comprehension and notes the shortcomings of traditional views of reading comprehension.

Smith, Frank. *Comprehension and Learning.* New York: Holt, Rinehart and Winston, 1975. Smith views comprehension as a cognitive psychologist and draws on both information-processing theory and psycholinguistic theory in his explanation of comprehension. This discussion of cognitive structure with attention to distinctive-feature learning should be part of a teacher's background in understanding the nature of comprehension in reading.

Smith, Frank. "The Role of Prediction in Reading," *Elementary English* 52 (March 1975): 305–11. Smith maintains that comprehension in both spoken and written language requires prediction, and he encourages teachers to encourage children to use prediction as an aid to critical reading as well as an aid to word identification.

Stauffer, Russell G. *Directing the Reading Thinking Process.* New York: Harper and Row, 1975. Stauffer details the use of the pupil-purpose setting procedure in chapter 2 of this lucid book, which stresses the view of reading-as-thinking throughout.

7

Linguistic Perspectives for Instruction

The perception of reading as a language-based process is one of the most important, if not the most important, major influence on reading theory in the past ten to twenty years. As theory changes and expands, so do instructional practices, although changes in practice based on theory may occur more slowly than new information appears. Modern research and theory on language and language learning should make it possible to develop a more adequate methodology for teaching reading.

This book represents an attempt to present information about the language base for reading. We have identified implications for instruction in the preceding material where appropriate. In this chapter we are focusing on the classroom with perspectives on the teacher's role in facilitating learning to read, on starting to read, on diagnosis and remediation, and on selected instructional strategies.

A Linguistic Perspective on the Teacher's Role in Facilitating Reading

Whenever significant learning occurs in a classroom, several factors are interacting favorably. These factors are related to the learner and his expectations about what is to be learned and to the teacher's assumptions about the nature of learning, the nature of language, and the nature of her role in the instruction. Wide differences persist regarding the appropriate assumptions a teacher should have.

It is our view that maximizing the opportunity for meaningful learning to occur results when learners are viewed as capable of learning, when language (especially as it relates to reading) is viewed as nonfragmentable, and when the teacher is supportive. It is unfortunate, but too often true, that teachers have seen a dichotomy between teaching and learning and have perceived their role as separate from the learning event. Postman and Weingartner captured the essence of this thinking when they quoted a teacher who stated, "Oh, I taught them that, but they didn't learn it." [1] They elaborated: "From our point of view, it is on the same level as a salesman's remarking 'I sold it to him, but he didn't buy it'—which is to say, it makes no sense. It seems to mean that 'teaching' is what a 'teacher' does, which, in turn, may or may not bear any relationship to what those being 'taught' do." [2]

As we view the role of the teacher in learning in general and learning to read in particular, we advocate a threefold set of tasks that we believe establishes an appropriate relationship between teaching and learning—between the teacher and the learner. First, the teacher must provide a learning environment in which what is to be learned is perceived by the learner as worth the expenditure of energy and effort and is worth risking the possibility of not succeeding at first. Second, the teacher must plan for, arrange, and involve learners in meaningful encounters with written language and must, within that, promote its communicative function throughout. And, third, the teacher must focus positively on the learner's efforts in learning to process written language by providing support and encouragement and by appreciating the learner's attempts.

That is to say, learning to read must not present bits and pieces of unrelated fragments of language or terminology that, although logical to an adult, may be both illogical and meaningless to the child. That what is to be learned is perceived by the learner as worth the effort involved requires a teacher role that focuses on the communicative and purposeful characteristics of written language processing in a meaning-getting context. It also requires that the teacher view mistakes as necessary to the learning process and, quite often, evidence that learning is occurring. As she plans written-language activities for her learners, she must emphasize her role as supportive, encouraging, and responsive to the risk-taking (and thus potential error-making) of the learner.

She should plan reading activities that help readers develop strategies for processing written language. She must plan these activities by adhering to a language-processing view of reading instruction and must help her students focus on getting meaning from written language materials related to their interests. She must also provide opportunities for independent, self-selected reading in order to ensure independence in reading.

Carl Rogers identified a number of principles of learning relevant to our concept of the teacher's role in reading instruction. Primary among these principles is his statement that "human beings have a natural potentiality for learning." [3] There is, according to Rogers, a basic curiosity about the world, a "desire for learning, for discovery, for enlargement of knowledge and experience which can be released under suitable conditions." [4] These conditions, Rogers went on to say, include learner participation

---

[1] Neil Postman and Charles Weingartner, *Teaching as a Subversive Activity* (New York: Dell Publishing Company, 1969), p. 37.

[2] *Ibid.*, p. 37.

[3] Carl R. Rogers, *Freedom to Learn* (Columbus, Ohio: Charles E. Merrill Publishing Company, 1969), p. 157.

[4] *Ibid.*, p. 158.

in the learning process, low threats to self, and relevant subject matter which involves both the feelings and the intellect of the learner.[5]

Nowhere is the potentiality for learning more dramatically demonstrated than in language acquisition. In an awesomely short period of time, children learn to control the highly complex system of language. Children learn this system under the freeing conditions Rogers postulated, and they do so with an eagerness and enthusiasm that can only be described as a spontaneous and energetic expectation that the system—language—is worth knowing. It is this eagerness and enthusiasm for learning that teachers must tap and relate to learning to read.

Frank Smith described a child's expectations of school, suggesting that a child arrives at school ready and willing to learn, and he expects that what he encounters at school will eventually make sense.[6] Smith identified the teacher's task as one of persuading the child that he is once again in an environment where learning is worth the trouble and risk involved and then finding situations in which the child succeeds at learning. Thus, learning requires that what is to be learned be potentially meaningful for the learner. When the learner perceives that the environment affords his sense-making strategies and that his efforts at learning are valued, his potentiality for learning will be released. On the other hand, when such sense-making efforts are unrewarded, ill-appreciated, or rejected, the learner may, in turn, reject both the environment and learning.

Accordingly, those responsible for teaching reading should consider themselves responsible not so much for "teaching" but rather for encouraging and valuing the learning process so natural to being human. In this perspective, teachers are responsible for providing relevant experiences in and with written language in a "free to learn" environment that encourages the learning of the structure of written language through an emphasis on the purposeful and communicative aspects of all language processing. The role is one of support, encouragement, enthusiasm and, to a large degree, one of arranging involvement in learning to read. Classroom teachers who adhere to these ideas will find they are more intimately involved with each learner and the learning process than those teachers who dichotomize teaching and learning.

A Linguistic Perspective on Starting to Read

The foundation for a successful start in reading is in large measure a linguistic foundation. Linguistic foundations for prereading and beginning reading encompass those linguistic factors which would influence success in the initial learning-to-read process. From a linguistic perspective, the level of readiness and beginning reading instruction is related to each child's background in linguistic performance and linguistic competence. An introduction to reading should help the beginner apply his familiarity with the spoken language and his language learning abilities to the learning of the written code.

Readiness for reading has long been thought of as a composite of factors and skills that influence a child's ability to learn to read successfully. Linguistic readiness has

[5]*Ibid.,* pp. 158–62.
[6]Frank Smith, *Comprehension and Learning* (New York: Holt, Rinehart and Winston, 1975), p. 226.

been one of the factors ordinarily included in discussions of readiness, but usually discussions of the language background have focused on a child's general ability to express and comprehend ideas in oral language and on the learner's listening and speaking vocabularies. Often, assumptions made about a child's linguistic readiness may have been erroneous and may have underestimated actual linguistic competence. Disadvantaged and linguistically different children were often misdiagnosed on the language factor. Most children come to school with sufficient linguistic background to understand the written language information in beginning reading materials are appropriately selected for their language and experiential backgrounds. Of course the language factor is not the only one in readiness for reading, but children should not be denied opportunities for learning because of wrong assumptions about their linguistic ability.

Teachers must recognize that all children who come to them in kindergarten and first grade are already users of language, although most children are not yet users of written language in reading and writing at the time of school entrance. Teachers must respect, accept, and build upon the language children bring with them to the school setting. The existing use of spoken language is the base for written language learning. The school instruction does not teach the oral language—that is known. What must be offered in school is the opportunity for language expansion and for instruction in written language learning. The language use and language learning ability, the insatiable curiosity of the young child about his world, and the momentum to continue to learn the learner brings with him can be the bridge to literacy.

A philosophical base for considering how teachers can assist in the learning of written language is provided when reading and writing are viewed as extensions of the process of language acquisition begun in infancy. The nature of the language learner, the nature of language, and the nature of language learning give clues about how a child learns to read. In oral language acquisition, the child is an active discoverer of the patterns of language as he uses that language to communicate and as he is immersed in a language environment. The learning environment for children in the prereading and beginning reading stages should be constructed to foster the child's active discovery of the nature and patterns of written language. All of the language learning ability a child exhibited in the learning of speech demonstrates the learner's ability for language learning. Reading is also a language learning task and one to which a learner brings remarkable power in language communication. The language processing nature of reading should be a major consideration in planning prereading and beginning reading experiences.

In prereading and beginning reading, it is essential for children to develop the basic concepts that reading is a form of communication and that written language represents meaning. To do this, the teacher can use children's oral language to create language experience materials. In prereading and beginning reading, children should have real language used in instructional materials within a meaningful communication setting. The abstractness of written language is a stumbling block for the child first learning to read. But that abstractness can be lessened if the content of the material is directly related to the learner as it is when it represents his own language and experience.

Exposure to written language is needed to provide readiness for reading. Exposure to print does not come after children learn to read; the exposure is needed to prepare children for reading. Many commercial reading readiness materials contain only limited exposure to written language. Perhaps even more significant is the lack of commercial readiness materials to present reading as a communication process. Not only in beginning reading but in the readiness stage as well, there should be natural and abundant exposure to written language so that the abstractness of the written code is lessened. Writing stories to correlate with children's art work, displaying meaningful captions on bulletin boards, creating books, and recording meaningful events with language experience stories can provide exposure to and create interest in written language as part of the total environment in preschool and kindergarten settings.

Through the written language-experience products, a thorough prereading and beginning reading program can be offered. In addition to showing the function of written language as a tool for communication, the recordings of children's dictation can be used to illustrate the skills of visual discrimination, visual memory, auditory discrimination, letter-name knowledge, and left-to-right progression, to develop language concepts, and to create interest in reading. As children match word, letter, phrase, and sentence cards to words, letters, phrases, and sentences in experience stories, they are acquiring the prereading skill of visual discrimination in a reading situation while they extend their concepts of these language units. As experience stories are read aloud to children, the left-to-right direction of writing can be demonstated easily. Auditory discrimination can be shown by focusing on selected examples of words from experience stories to illustrate the idea of similarities and differences in beginning and rhyming sounds.

No sharp dividing line should exist between prereading and beginning reading. As Durkin has so aptly noted, what is for some children a prereading experience is for other children beginning reading.[7] By using language experience materials and activities it is possible to blend prereading and beginning reading. The learners will indicate through rereading and follow-up activities in word matching, sentence building, and others when they can begin to acquire a reading vocabulary and to start to read successfully.[8]

In the beginning-to-read instruction, the setting for learning to read should be one which presents the learner with meaningful language and plausible content so that comprehension is regarded as important by teacher and student and so that all the cue systems of the language can be processed. The setting for the introduction to reading should also permit the learner to discover the patterns of the orthographic system that are useful in reading and spelling. However, attention to the graphophonic cues should not obscure comprehension.

Learning to read represents a significant intellectual achievement. Learning to read is highly valued in our culture, and the high value placed on learning to read may result in some distorted instructional emphases and may create great pressures on some learners. What should be a pleasurable personal discovery can become a torturous failure. Success for the learner should be the highest priority in beginning reading programs with a strong language base.

---

[7]Dolores Durkin, *Teaching Them to Read* (Boston: Allyn and Bacon, 1974), pp. 128, 131.

[8]MaryAnne Hall, *Teaching Reading as a Language Experience* (Columbus, Ohio: Charles E. Merrill Publishing Company, 1976).

A Linguistic Prespective for Diagnosis and Correction

The plight of the "poor" reader has been of concern to educators and society in general as well as to parents and the readers themselves. Traditionally a reader has been evaluated as unsuccessful if there is a lack of achievement in relation to ability and/or grade level expectations. Standardized tests as well as specific diagnostic tests have been widely employed to provide information on which to base evaluation and examination of reading achievement. Examination of an individual's reading ability must include an analysis of his language processing abilities.

Since we view reading as a holistic meaning-getting process that involves the application of various strategies to the cue systems of written language, our view of assessment of growth of reading proficiency requires examination of the relative effectiveness of the reader's use of reading strategies to obtain meaning. Consequently, assessment procedures which focus on the reader's effectiveness in obtaining meaning from written language rather than procedures that place a premium on precision in isolated aspects of the reading process would be utilized.

We have suggested throughout this book that learning to read requires learning to process the written language symbols that represent meaning. That learning may require the learner to induce his own rule system for the structure of written language and develop a variety of strategies for making use of that system. For a variety of reasons, some children may become more proficient than others in their use of reading strategies with regular classroom instruction. Planning effective instructional activities so as to provide optimum opportunity for all learners to become proficient readers requires that teachers know what strategies their students as a group and as individuals are using. To determine the strategies used by a reader requires some form of assessment or testing procedure. However, not all procedures are equally compatible with a linguistic perspective for reading.

A central issue in all assessment is validity. Test validity is a term used to refer to whether or not a particular procedure measures what it claims to measure. Reading tests should test the construct *reading*: composition tests should test the construct *composition*, etc. The test tasks or test items used to assess the construct under examination should accurately and adequately reflect that construct. When the items do not reflect the construct accurately, the test is not "construct valid."

Unfortunately, use of tests has often been based upon little or no examination of test validity. As a consequence, spelling tasks have sometimes been considered aspects of reading ability, and some children may have been considered poor *readers* as a result. Critical examination of tests and testing procedures is necessary and crucial to the success of evaluation. Unexamined procedures may lead to inappropriate interpretations and, possibly, to false assumptions about children and what they know or can do. Accurately reflecting the construct under examination is essential in assessment; reading tests must assess reading.

From a language-processing perspective, reading assessment can only occur when one examines what reading strategies a reader uses and how he makes use of the cue systems of written language. Assessment of this nature occurs when a reader is reading whole language in a context, such as oral reading, in which inferences regarding his strategies and use of the cue systems can be made.

One procedure for obtaining information regarding a reader's use of the reading process is qualitative analysis of a reader's oral reading from a language-processing perspective. Under the initial direction of Kenneth Goodman, work in applied psycholinguistics has led to the creation of a procedure for inferring reading proficiency from oral reading samples. In this procedure, deviations from the text that occur during oral reading (*miscues*[9]) are analyzed in order to infer the reader's strategies.[10] It is assumed that all readers deviate from the text and that evaluation of these deviations can allow the evaluator to draw conclusions regarding the effectiveness of the reader's strategies. It is also assumed that since meaning is the goal in reading, some lack of precision in word identification is to be expected. Readers actively process written language to obtain the message encoded in the written language, not to accurately identify each and every individual word.

Analysis of oral reading miscues based on the degree to which the meaning of the text is disrupted allows a teacher to evaluate reading proficiency and subsequently permits her to develop appropriate instructional activites. The *Reading Miscue Inventory* (RMI)[11] is a published procedure for analyzing oral reading miscues. The *RMI* procedure consists of obtaining an oral reading sample and then qualitatively analyzing each of the reader's miscues through a series of questions about the miscue. Miscues are assumed to be a natural part of the reading process for all readers, but some miscues can be qualitatively better than others. Meaning getting may be interrupted by some miscues, but not by others. Miscues that do not interfere with acquiring meaning may, in fact, be evidence of reader proficiency rather than ineffectiveness.

For example, in the sentence *As the car behind them began to speed up, Benjie and Bobby thought they were being chased down the road*, miscues such as *Benny* for *Benjie* or *street* for *road* would probably not affect the reader's search for meaning, whereas miscues such as *chose* for *chased* and *rod* for *road* probably would. If a reader evidenced the miscue *street* for *road*, the explanation might be: Since *street* may be a more familiar term than *road* for the concept anticipated by the reader through the context, the miscue evidences both effective sampling (not identifying every word or every letter of a word) and predicting (eliminating words that do not make sense syntactically or semantically) strategies. Processing for meaning not accuracy in word perception is effective reading.

This linguistic perspective for examination of a reader's use of the reading process based on qualitative miscue analysis may change present practices for identifying reading "difficulties," selecting "poor" readers for diagnostic and corrective efforts, and planning and carrying out corrective/remedial reading programs. Basing an analysis of a reader's use of the reading process solely on quantitatively analyzed reading errors implies that accuracy in word perception is paramount and that each deviation from the text is equal to every other. The result of such analysis has been an emphasis on precision and accuracy rather than on language-processing. This emphasis has, in turn, spawned referrals for "remedial reading" for children who,

---

[9]Kenneth S. Goodman, "The Reading Process: Theory and Practice," in Richard Hodges and E. Hugh Rudorf, eds., *Language and Learning to Read: What Teachers Should Know About Language* (Boston: Houghton-Mifflin Co., 1972), p. 147.

[10]Yetta M. Goodman and Carolyn L. Burke, *Reading Miscue Inventory, Manual, Procedure for Diagnosis and Evaluation* (New York: The Macmillan Company, 1972), p. 5.

[11]*Ibid.*

although lacking in precision and accuracy in word perception, clearly processed the written language symbols in a meaningful manner.

In our view, miscues should be expected since they are natural aspects of a active search for meaning. Identification of reading difficulties from this perspective, then, would be focused on the effects of miscues on obtaining meaning. Selection of "poor" readers for diagnostic and corrective procedures would be made by analyzing patterns of miscues made by readers. Only those readers who appear to make poor use of written language-processing strategies would be involved in a program of continuing diagnosis and correction. Readers whose miscues evidence effective meaning-getting strategies, even though precision in word identification might under other assumptions be considered a reading "problem," would *not* be selected for corrective/remedial programs. Readers who evidence difficulty in achieving effectiveness in written language processing strategies rather than readers who "do not know phonics" or "can't syllabicate words correctly" or "omit too many words in their reading" would be selected for additional diagnostic procedures and perhaps correction/remediation.

However, the nature of corrective/remedial teaching would differ in few respects from teaching that adhered to our suggestions in chapters 5 and 6. We do not view the nature of corrective/remedial instruction as qualitatively different from other reading instruction if that instruction is linguistically and psychologically sound. Individual learners may need different sorts of experiences and the same learner may need different experiences at different stages in his development toward reading proficiency, but good reading instruction implies planning for and meeting these varying needs *at all times*.

There are some learners who are ineffective readers and for those children who are ineffective users of the reading process, increased emphasis should be placed on demonstrating appropriate strategies working from the reader's strengths. And, at all times, especially for readers who have not had successful experiences with written language, corrective/remedial instruction in reading must be planned to focus on developing in the reader the concept of the communicative function of written language and must be carried out through meaningful written language experiences.

Assessment of growth in reading ability and diagnosis and correction of reading difficulties from a linguistic perspective means defining reading as a language processing activity in which miscueing is to be expected, assessing growth and conducting diagnosis in terms of qualitatively analyzing patterns of miscues for the purpose of conceiving and planning appropriate reading instruction, and carrying our corrective/remedial instruction so that it is compatible with the needs of the individual. If teachers of reading facilitate learning to read in an atmosphere of sensitive encouragement by helping children make use of the learning strategies they already possess and by providing written language experiences in which reading strategies may be developed, the need for intensive diagnostic evaluation and extensive corrective/remedial programs, will, in our opinion, be greatly diminished.

Selected Instructional Strategies with a Linguistic Foundation

All reading is linguistic since the act of reading requires the processing of language for communication. Some instructional strategies capitalize on the linguistic, communicative function of reading; others do not. Effective reading instruction should be based on helping readers master and apply the linguistic processing tasks effective reading demands. The applications of the linguistic foundations for instruction are both broad and numerous. The strategies highlighted here are those that stand out as having considerable linguistic rationale; however, these are only a few examples of instructional precedures based on the linguistic nature of the reading process. In the examples discussed below, the importance of meaning is evident. Also apparent is the use of meaningful instead of fragmented language in order to teach reading as the reconstruction of messages from print.

The Language Experience Approach

The instructional approach with perhaps the strongest linguistic rationale is the language experience approach. This approach for teaching reading is based on the creation of reading materials by writing children's spoken thoughts. Hall explained, "The essence of the language experience approach is the use of the language and thinking of the learner as a foundation for reading instruction."[12] Materials created by the learners, no vocabulary controls, and the integration of all the language arts are characteristics of this method. Although this approach has its greatest application in the prereading and beginning reading stages of instruction, it can be applied selectively for students needing corrective or remedial help, and can be used with other methods as well as being used in conjunction with language programs to further creativity and fluency in written expression.

The linguistic rationale for this approach is evident since:

1. The relationship between spoken and written language is clearly shown.
2. The language of reading materials corresponds closely to the reader's spoken language.
3. The purpose of reading and writing as tools of communication is central.
4. Meaningful units of language incorporating all three cue systems of the language are featured.
5. The linguistic performance and competence of each language learner are respected and used to further development in reading and other language communication.
6. The other language processes of listening, speaking, reading, and writing are integrated with reading.
7. Intonation cues can be an aid to the reader since he is reading material that was first spoken.

In addition to the linguistic reasons for advocating language-experience reading instruction, there is a well-founded psychological rationale for this approach. The factors of personal and active involvement, creativity, attitude, success, motivation, and interest contribute to learning. Language experience reading when well done helps learners discover how the written language system operates as they are actively involved in the use of that system in personal communicative efforts. Language experience instruction is a nonthreatening learning situation and for this reason is

---

[12]MaryAnne Hall, *Teaching Reading as a Language Experience* (Columbus, Ohio: Charles E. Merrill Publishing Company, 1976), p. 1.

often very appropriate for the student who has been unsuccessful with other approaches.

The procedures to be followed in the development and use of student-created reading materials in language-experience reading instruction generally include motivation and oral discussion prior to recording children's language. After language-experience materials are produced, selected reading and other follow-up activities will be conducted. Throughout the instruction, the language and thinking of the learner will be accepted, and the procedures employed should capitalize on the naturalness of language learning. Children's vocabulary and syntax will not be changed, but standard spelling will be used.

The following story is one example of a group-experience story composed by a group of first-grade inner-city students who had not yet started to read. These children were considered "very disadvantaged and nonverbal" by their teacher who had requested help from a resource teacher.

The Terrible Monster

Marilet said, "The monster is so ugly."
Cedric said, "He has long teeth."
Dwayne said, "He has a long nose."
Henry said, "He is big and he can eat people and he can eat the school."
Tyrone said, "That monster mean."

The procedures followed with this language experience example were those stated previously. The motivation consisted of reading the book, *Where the Wild Things Are* by Maurice Sendak[13] to the group. Oral discussion followed. In that discussion, most of the children's comments dealt with monsters. The children decided to write a story about a monster. The next step was for the teacher to write children's comments. After this a title was selected by the group. The teacher then read the story *to* the group, and then the teacher read the story *with* the group orally. Then each child read the sentence he or she had contributed *with* the teacher. Reading language experience stories *to* and *with* children is recommended since in the prereading and beginning reading stages children should not feel frustrated by being asked to read something independently if they can not yet do this. After the reading of the story, the lesson for the first day was complete. The next day the teacher displayed the chart story and again read it to and with the children. Children volunteered to read the story or sentences independently. For follow-up activities children matched word, phrase, and sentence cards to words, phrases, and sentences on the chart for visual discrimination practice. The third day children were given a dittoed copy of the story. This story was the first of many kept in folders, which then became one kind of reading book for these children. When children get dittoed copies they can illustrate the stories and can underline the words that they know how to read. The known words are then part of the word banks children keep in the language experience approach to learning to read. The group which composed the monster story also created a group book composed of pages by each individual of an illustration of a monster and a dictated story.

---

[13]Maurice Sendak, *Where the Wild Things Are* (New York: Harper and Row, 1963).

The follow-up activities will vary according to the level and needs of each group. For example, in prereading the attention may be more on oral language expression, visual discrimination, auditory discrimination, and left-to-right progression than on the acquisition of a reading vocabulary, which is very important in initial reading instruction. For beginning readers, selected examples to illustrate certain consonant phoneme-grapheme correspondences or other graphophonic information could be used from the same materials.

Whenever language experience programs are used, the content must be related to and drawn from the learners. The language of the learners is the base from which further language learning stems. Language experience programs provide extensive opportunities for creative writing and for oral communication. In a language experience classroom, children's writing is valued and is displayed attractively.

THE CLOZE PROCEDURE

Another instructional strategy that has a linguistic base is the *cloze procedure*. In cloze activities, reading material is presented in a form with a pattern of systematic word deletions. Since the introduction of the cloze procedure in 1953 by Taylor,[14] it has been widely used to measure the readability of passages. In recent years, cloze activities have been used instructionally in connection with vocabulary and comprehension. The use of semantic and syntactic clues can be emphasized with cloze activities.

The following is an example of a cloze passage. As you think of appropriate words for the blanks, notice your dependence on semantic and syntactic cues.

The popularity of tennis has reached an all-time high in the United States. This active sport _____ caught on with young _____ old alike. While the _____ may still have private _____ and may belong to _____ clubs, tennis is no _____ just a rich man's _____. Neighborhood tennis facilities are _____ available for the average _____. Ever increasing numbers of tennis _____ are proclaiming the marvelous _____ of the game. Tennis _____?

The customary pattern for cloze exercises is that of every fifth word deleted. The every fifth word deletion pattern is the pattern employed when the purpose of cloze activities is to estimate readability. When the purpose of cloze activities is to teach language structure clues and vocabulary extension, the deletion pattern can be altered according to purpose and according to the level of individual readers.

A variation of the cloze procedure is to have children brainstorm for all the possible words which will fit in each blank. This procedure is recommended for vocabulary enrichment and also can help alert students to the effect of individual words on meaning of a sentence or passage and can also show the effect of context on the meaning of a word. Discussion of all suggested possibilities for a blank provides opportunities for discussion of synonyms as well as for discovering that words supplied must be syntactically appropriate. Another adaptation is to underline words in an intact passage and

---

[14]Wilson L. Taylor "Cloze Procedure: A New Tool for Measuring Readability," *Journalism Quarterly* 30 (Fall, 1953):415–33.

have children change the underlined word to a word with an opposite meaning. One creative teacher had students change selected words in magazine ads to words with opposite meanings with excellent results in interest and vocabulary development.

An additional modification of the cloze procedure is to delete a selected category of word such as adjectives, nouns, or verbs in a passage. (Children do not have to use this terminology.) As students discuss possibilities for each blank, they can realize that the function of the suggested words is the same.

Another application of the cloze procedure is to work with the structure or function words of language by deleting these words from a paragraph. When words such as *but, as, while* and other connectives are deleted, children can learn how these words serve to indicate that there is often a relatedness between the parts of a sentence they connect. Lack of accurate interpretation of interrelated ideas can be one cause of faulty comprehension.

The cloze procedure can be also used to provide practive with inflected forms. A paragraph in which words with inflectional endings are deleted can be used, and as the answers are discussed children can discover and state how the context determined which form of a word would be appropriate. This type of practice with endings seems more related to the task of reading than does the common practice of having children work with words in isolation as they add endings in a situation which is unlike the actual reading task.

Still another modification of the cloze idea is to use selections in which the first letter or letter cluster for the deleted word is given. This variation can be useful for combining graphophonic cues with syntactic and contextual ones.

We advocate the use of cloze activities since these activities deal with vocabulary and language structure in a contextual reading situation. Although cloze activities seem to be an excellent vehicle for combining semantic and syntactical clues, this activity should not be overemphasized so that it becomes repetitive drill. The bulk of instructional time should be spent on meaningful reading of both fictional or factual contextual material.

READING-THINKING STRATEGIES

In the next few pages are illustrations of instruction that focus on the written-language processing strategies of predicting, confirming, and comprehending. These strategies involve both divergent and convergent thinking as well as reflective affect-involving interaction with and reaction to the author's message. At all times a reader should be actively involved in employing a variety of strategies to process written language into meaningful interpretations. To become effective in these intellectual activities readers need teacher guidance and support and the opportunity to develop these strategies.

Reading-as-process implies a wholeness—a set of interrelationships among aspects of the process—that does not lend itself to divisability. Aspects of the reading process examined or taught separately lose essential characteristics they held in the whole of the process. Isolating an aspect of the reading process for the purpose of teaching it may not only change its nature; it may also make learning more difficult. According to Yetta Goodman, "To isolate units of language and teach them directly to readers confuses learning and increases complexity, for it creates a more abstract task for readers than they face in whole language."[15] Instructional activities that promote effective use of the reading process do not fragment language or isolate aspects of the process. Rather, effective strategies for processing written language are developed through selected emphasis on various aspects of the reading process in whole, meaningful language to arrive at meaningful interpretation.

Compatible with this conceptualization of reading instruction are strategy lessons[16] and directed-reading-thinking activities.[17] Strategy lessons are planned reading situations in which the use of selected reading strategies are highlighted by encouraging the reader to make conscious use of the selected strategies in a specifically prepared written language context.[18] Through emphasis on developing a selected strategy in a natural language context rather than isolating a skill and teaching it in fragments of language, readers learn to use simultaneously all the cues in written language. An essential characteristic of such strategy lessons is the whole language context in which meaningfulness is high and ambiguity, which is the result of isolation or fragmentation, is low.

One of the strategies used by effective readers is the strategy of prediction. Frank Smith defined prediction as "the prior elimination of unlikely alternatives."[19] He argued that prediction goes on for all of us at all times because we are constantly predicting what we will see next, what we will hear next, etc., in every context in which we find ourselves. Because we encounter familiar situations most of the time, we reduce the range of possible events in similar contexts to those we expect due to prior experience. Looking out of a window in June in Georgia, one would expect to see a number of things but certainly not snow. Thus, one would not predict snow; it would be contextually eliminated.

Effective readers apply predicting strategies to their encounters with written language, reducing or eliminating unlikely alternatives as they process the message. Prediction in reading may be illustrated by the following sentence "When she fell on the pavement, she scraped her _____." Most of us would complete the sentence with *knee* or *hand* or perhaps *elbow*. Syntactic and semantic constraints reduce the range of alternatives, enabling the elimination of those which are syntactically or semantically unlikely.

Another strategy that readers can use is the strategy of confirming. Confirming occurs as the reader tests his predictions against subsequent information. Effective readers ask themselves whether what they are reading "sounds like language" and whether it "makes sense." Effective readers also exhibit the strategy of regressing or rereading if they are unable to confirm their predictions.

A modified cloze procedure passage in which a single word, repeated a number of times in a passage, is deleted each time it appears, may be used to help readers learn to predict and confirm as they read. Such a passage may look like this:

---

[15]Yetta M. Goodman, "Reading Strategy Lessons: Expanding Reading Effectiveness," in William Page, ed., *Help for the Reading Teacher: New Directions in Research* (Urbana, Illinois: Eric Clearinghouse on Reading and Communication Skills, 1975), p. 35.

[16]Yetta M. Goodman, Carolyn L. Burke and Barry Sherman, *Strategies in Reading* (New York: Macmillan Publishing Company, 1975).

[17]Russell G. Stauffer, *Directing the Reading Thinking Process* (New York: Harper and Row, 1975).

[18]Yetta M. Goodman and Carolyn M. Burke, *Reading Miscue Inventory, Manual, Procedure for Diagnosis and Evaluation* (New York: The Macmillan Company, 1972), p. 97.

[19]Frank Smith, "The Role of Prediction in Reading" *Elementary English* 52 (March, 1975):306.

Like many other sports _____appears to be increasingly higher paying for those who play it. Contracts for _____players are now nearing the $100,000 per year level on the average with the "better" _____ players receiving as much as $200,000 a year or more. A team with half or more of its twelve members getting paid the $100,000 a year average must allocate $600,000 or more for those players' salaries alone. And since most of these_____ teams must travel from such places as Boston to Phoenix, travel must also be a rather large budget allocation.

Of course, compared to football with its equipment costs and large player roster, baseball with its extensive farm system and long season, and hockey with its constant need for "good ice", _____ may seem an advantageous investment for someone looking for a place to put some of his millions.

A teacher could present the first paragraph of this passage to a student or group of students and ask for their predictions for the word omitted. She could then present subsequent portions of the passage again eliciting additional guesses and focusing on how such predictions were derived and how these predictions can be confirmed. For example, the teacher might use the phrase "like many other sports" to show that the content of the passage is restricted to sports. She might then obtain a list of sports that could be used in the blank. Next, the teacher might direct attention to the words "higher paying" and "contracts" and the monetary figures to help the learners reduce the range of possibilities to professional sports. The size of the team, indicated by the phrase "half of its twelve members," further reduces the possibilities. The final paragraph compares the unknown sport to three other major professional sports, limiting the possibility to *basketball*.

The emphasis throughout the lesson is on making predictions, examining these predictions in light of subsequent information, and omitting those that do not meet the constraints imposed by the logic and language of the passage. By demonstrating prediction, discussing the thinking underlying how the predictions were formulated, and emphasizing the use of written language cues, teachers can help readers learn to make use of predicting and confirming strategies.

Beyond the predicting and confirming aspects of the reading process is comprehending. Comprehending is related to one's purpose for reading and one's previous experience with the topic. Questions like "What should be remembered?" "What do I agree/disagree with?" and "How does this relate to what I already know?" are related to comprehending strategies. Effective readers are critical readers who ask relevant questions, process ideas according to purposes, and make judgments while reading. Helping children learn to be effective, critical readers who examine, hypothesize, find proof, suspend judgment and make decisions (who think) can be accomplished through the sort of directed reading-thinking activities advocated by Stauffer.[20]

A directed reading-thinking activity begins with a teacher guiding a group of children in the examination of a portion (perhaps the title and/or some pictures) of a story or other material and asking them to speculate about the content through such questions as: "What do you think a story or selection with a title like this will be about?" or "What could happen in this story?" Each child's response to such ques-

---

[20]Russell G. Stauffer, *Directing the Reading Thinking Process* (New York: Harper and Row, 1975), p. 70.

tioning becomes, in effect, his purpose for reading, the hypothesis for which he attempts to gather support by reading. Stauffer says of the reader in D-R-T-A's, "He must raise the questions and to him belongs the challenge and the responsibility of a judgment."[21]

The teacher next asks her students to silently read some portion of the story in search of evidence relative to the purposes established in the discussion. When the reading is completed, she may ask "Now, what do you think?" or "Now, what do you think will happen next?" in order to promote the use of the information obtained in this first segment of reading for making new inferences. Or, the teacher may ask, "Were you right?" or "Was it what you expected?" in order to focus on evaluation of the original hypothesis. At this point, she may ask some of the readers to find portions of the text that support their original hypothesis and read those portions aloud. This kind of purposeful, motivated oral reading is reader-initiated rather than teacher-fabricated and is expressive instead of word-by-word since it is done to prove points.[22]

Following this discussion, further speculation about events and plot may ensue with attention drawn to additional pictures or portions of the story. Again, after the children have read more of the story the teacher may ask questions similar to those asked earlier.

The length of portions to be read as well as the purposes for which reading is done should vary according to the nature of the material and according to the maturity of the reader. Different types of material, variation in cues used to establish purposes and differing amounts of reading are necessary variations which will enhance reader effectiveness. Varying the demands in these ways fosters reader-thinking flexibility and ultimately improves the quality of judgments made during the reading-thinking process.[23] In D-R-T-A's readers use the reading process to gather support for their hypotheses. The purposeful nature of such use of the reading process demands whole, natural and substantive language.

Both strategy lessons and directed reading-thinking activities treat reading as a holistic meaning-getting process. This is, we believe, an essential characteristic of linguistically sound reading instruction.

Concluding Statement

Reading is a language-based process, and the teaching of reading should be based on valid information about language and language learning. The teacher of reading and other communication processes needs to be informed about the workings of the language code as she provides a setting in which children become readers. There is promise for improved learning and teaching of reading as the teacher's understanding of the linguistic foundations for reading increases. There is promise for improved learning and teaching of reading as materials and procedures have an accurate linguistic base coupled with sound pedagogy. There is promise for improved learning and teaching of reading as each child's language learning capacities are respected and

---

[21]*Ibid.*, p. 37.
[22]*Ibid.*, p. 47.
[23]*Ibid.*, p. 42.

extended. There is promise for improved learning and teaching of reading too through future research on the language-processing nature of reading.

Suggested Readings

Bormuth, John. "The Cloze Readability Procedure," *Elementary English* 45 (April 1968): 429–36. A very detailed description for using the cloze procedure as a readability measure is given here.

Durkin, Dolores. *Teaching Young Children to Read.* Boston: Allyn and Bacon, 1976. Durkin provides much detail on readiness for reading from consideration both of factors in the child and of factors in instruction.

Goodman, Yetta M. and Carolyn L. Burke. *Reading Miscue Inventory Manual Procedure for Diagnosis and Evaluation.* New York: The Macmillan Co., 1972. This source is recommended for those interested in studying the reading miscue diagnostic procedures in detail. The assumptions about the reading process give a view of reading as a psycholinguistic process.

Farr, Roger, *Reading: What Can Be Measured?* Newark, Delaware: International Reading Association, 1969. For those interested in measurement and evaluation problems in reading, Farr's book is a source which is widely cited and readable. A guide to major tests in reading is included. Especially noteworthy is Farr's summary chapter.

Goodman, Kenneth S., ed. *Miscue Analysis: Applications to Reading Instruction.* Urbana, Illinois: Clearinghouse on Reading and Communications Skills, 1973. This collection of articles based on the use of miscue analysis may be found useful by those seeking specific examples of the nature of reading instruction derived from this perspective.

Hall, MaryAnne. *Teaching Reading as a Language Experience.* Columbus: Charles E. Merrill Publishing Company, 1976. This paperback book presents both theoretical rationale and descriptions of classroom implementation of the language experience approach. Great attention is given to the approach in prereading and beginning reading.

Hodges, Richard and E. Hugh Rudorf. *Language and Learning to Read.* Houghton-Mifflin Company, 1972. A central theme of this book is that teachers need to understand the nature of reading as language processing and to also understand the relationship of children's use of language to their reading performance.

Kean, John M., and Carl Personke. *The Language Arts: Teaching and Learning in the Elementary School.* New York: St. Martin's Press, 1976. Based on the premise that teachers of the English language arts must have a background in language and how it is learned, the authors devote one of three parts of their book to providing such necessary information. Part two deals with specific areas of the elementary language arts curriculum, and part three reflects a perspective for the language arts curriculum as a whole.

Moffett, James. *A Student-Centered Language Arts Curriculum, Grades K–13: A Handbook for Teachers.* Boston: Houghton-Mifflin, 1973, 1968. Moffett's book describes language activities for a wide range of growth stages and integrates all areas of the language arts. Of greatest concern to Moffett is attention to the learner and his language as the foundation for further growth in language.

Otto, Wayne, Richard A. McMenemy, and Richard J. Smith. *Corrective and Remedial Teaching* (2nd Edition). Boston: Houghton-Mifflin, 1973. For those interested in an examination of diagnosis and correction of reading difficulties, this book is recommended. Of special note are the emphasis on purposeful, meaningful reading instruction within a remedial setting and the authors' focus on reading as an affective as well as cognitive activity.

Page, William D., ed. *Help for the Reading Teacher: New Directions in Research.* Urbana, Illinois: National Conference on Research in English, 1975. Eight papers founded in a language-processing view of reading are collected in this short book. Included are implications for classroom practice derived from research in language and reading.

Pikulski, John J. "Using the Cloze Technique," *Language Arts* 53 (March 1976):317–18, 328. Pikulski gives a number of suggestions for using the cloze procedure as a teaching tool.

Smith, Richard J., and Thomas C. Barrett. *Teaching Reading in the Middle Grades.* Reading, Massachusetts: Addison-Wesley, 1974. Smith and Barrett provide useful information to teachers of middle grade (fourth through eighth) students in this highly readable text. Noteworthy are their consideration of affective responses to reading, of the use of reading to foster creativity, and of the transfer to content area reading.

Index